St. Azi

FURIOUS OBSERVATIONS OF A BLUE-EYED OJIBWAY:

Funny, You Don't Look Like One ~~Two~~ Three

FURIOUS OBSERVATIONS OF A BLUE-EYED OJIBWAY:

Funny, You Don't Look Like One ~~Two~~ Three

By Drew Hayden Taylor

Theytus Books Ltd.
Penticton B.C.
Canada

National library of Canada Cataloguing in Publication Data

Taylor, Drew Hayden, 1962
    Furious observations of a blue eyed Ojibway

    ISBN 1-894778-03-0

    1. Indians of North America--Canada--Humor   I.   Title.
II.   Title: Funny, you don't look like one III.
PS8589.A885F865   2002   C814'.54   C2002-910485-8
PR9199.3.T35F865   2002

Editorial: Greg Young-Ing and Leanne Flett
Cover photo: Dawn T. Maracle
Design: Leanne Flett
Proofing: Chick Gabriel

Theytus Books Ltd.
Lot 45, Green Mountain Rd.
RR#2, Site 50, Comp.8
Penticton, BC
V2A 6J7

Printed in Canada

*The publisher ackowledges the support of The Canada Council
for the Arts, The Department of Canadian Heritage and The
British Columbia Arts Council.*

CONTENTS

Introduction

OPINIONS!
(Who Gives a Flying....!)

GETTING THE N.A.C.
(*Native Artistic Community)

IDENTITY
(Stuff Psychiatrists Will Love)

LET ME TELL YOU ABOUT MY FRIENDS AND FAMILY...
(Be Afraid... Be Very Afraid!)

THE PLACES I'VE BEEN, THE THINGS I'VE SEEN
(An Aboriginal Travel Guide)

INTRODUCTION

Welcome to book three. Way back when, I never thought there would be a book # 1, let alone a third. But then again, I've never been that good at predicting the future. I have enough trouble with the present.

Not much has changed in the time between those 3 books... except for the fact that I now get a heck of a lot more letters and emails, telling me what an idiot I just might be. For example, in the past few years I have gotten letters from people reacting to my astonishment about the popularity of golf in the Native community, some saying I write about my former girlfriends way too much, one telling me I'm not dark enough to call myself a Native person, and still others telling me I'm not funny and to quit trying. Now that last one hurt.

Be that as it may, what started as an irritated rant in a newspaper over ten years ago, has now born it's third litter. What you are about to read are the best of the articles I have written over the past 3 years, opinions and observations that have appeared in *Windspeaker*, AFN'S *The Messenger*, *Now Magazine*, CBC Radio, *The Toronto Star*, *The Globe and Mail*, APTN*, Prairie Dog Magazine* and *New West Magazine,* just to name a few.

And in those dozen years of writing, one enormous fact that continues to astound me is how much the complex world of Native literature has grown and developed. There used to be just a few of us grinding up trees, just to share our imagination. But today, novels, plays, movies and music all seem to be growing at an exponential rate. Who knows what the next ten years will bring. I just hope the world will still be a fun and interesting place for book # 4. It better be or I'm out of a job and sleeping on your couch.

And on the eve of the publishing of this third book of ideas and commentaries, I am struck by 2 more impressions when looking at it's cover; the first being how much weight I've put on over the years and second, every time I think I've run out of something to say, some politician, an ex-girlfriend or the guy next to me on the bus would appear and give me a whole new batch of things to say. Somebody up there definitely likes me.

With that being said, I would like to send out a thank you to everybody in the world that I have had the privilege to meet, because by their very existence, they have inspired me to write. There's an old writer's proverb that says "In order to be a story-teller, you must first listen. In order to be a writer, you must first read." I would like to add something to that... and please feel free to quote me, "In order to be a snarky writer who thinks he's funny, watch the world like you are invisible." I'm sure truer words were never spoken, at least not in my house.

But perhaps a Blood Elder put it best in describing why I do what I do (instead of getting that job at the Band Office like my mother wanted), he said "Humour is the WD-40 of healing." In that case, maybe my mother will be happy if I tell her I'm trying to be a doctor...

So enjoy the book and if you get the chance, let me know if the material inside makes you laugh or angry. Hey, it may be worth an article.

OPINIONS!
(Who Gives a Flying.......!)

IS "PROFESSIONALISM" A DIRTY WORD?

Not that long ago I was in Tulsa, Oklahoma to attend the opening of a play of mine by a community Native theatre company located there. The director was a lovely and talented white woman who had been in theatre for a number of years. During our discussions that followed, she revealed that she had been having trouble with some, if not most, of the Native actors arriving on time and staying at rehearsal for any extended period of time. As a former Artistic Director of a Native theatre company, she asked me if this lack of professionalism was a common and understood practice in Native Theatre.

The good news, I told her, was that up in Canada, most of the Native actors I knew understood the concept of professionalism. Indian Time doesn't exist when other people are waiting for you and paying your cheque. The bad news was, it was an issue that extends much further than just the Native arts community. Doing your job well and professionally is an issue that is still having difficulty finding a home in many parts of our lives. And what gets me is in the short term, being sloppy may be easier, but in reality, it's not that difficult to do a good job or be on time.

Granted this is a topic that extends far beyond the Native community but I have found myself too many times trying to understand why people do what they do or explain this annoying factor to others. You'd think doing your job responsibly would be a naturally occurring work ethic. Living on the land and historically surviving in this country was difficult to those who didn't know what they were doing. The difference between life and death, as many Native hunters and fishermen will tell you, comes down to being responsible in your actions. I know too many Native people who are proud of the hours they put in and what finished product they come up with.

But I also remember during my time at Native Earth Performing Arts, having one director from the States tell me that several days into rehearsal one actor would continually come in late, then leave two hours early (cause he had another job to get to which he had neglected to inform us before we hired him). I asked the director if he wanted to fire the guy and he looked generally surprised, "I just assumed that was the way it was in Native theatre" he told me. We fired the guy. That saved him the trouble of having to show up every day.

Another time, a playwright showed up three days late for workshopping his play. He had not called or contacted the office in any way. Instead, the actors just sat there for three days, reading and rereading the script, wondering where the writer was. And when he finally arrived, he promptly wanted to be paid the full salary before starting the workshop. Needless to say, we did not end up workshopping his play or giving him his cheque. Hell has no fury like a peeved playwright; except a peeved Artistic Director.

And as I said, this is not a practice that is limited just to the arts community. Recently, there was a front page story in one of the national newspapers detailing the exorbitant salaries and perks many Chiefs and Councils from poverty stricken Reserves pay themselves annually. I believe, and don't quote me on this, one Chief got well over $400,000 a year! What the hell do you have to spend over $400,000 on in a poverty stricken Reserve? A better class of mongrel? Carpeted potholes? Heineken instead of a Labatt's Blue? The Betty Ford Clinic instead of the Pedahbun or Poundmaker Lodge.

Even the academic circles are forgetting the concept of professionalism. I know a woman who taught a course in Aboriginal Studies at a Toronto university, who is getting her hands slapped because she dared to be professional. Three Native students complained about their marks for substandard reasons. The first student attended half her classes but felt that she should get marked for FULL attendance. I think she said she was there in spirit. Or she wanted to be there but her dog ate her flat tire. Or she was there but invisible. Or something. The second failed to hand in six assignments but wanted credit for them anyway. I guess the idea of handing in those assignments was too radical an idea for a third year student. The third student wanted her grades raised simply because she was on academic probation and she was in danger of being kicked out. Evidently these students wanted to have their bannock and eat it too. And worst of all, the program coordinator and woman in charge of the Native Students Services both supported the students requests for higher marks, and attempted to change the marks without the instructors consent. I don't believe this is kosher – except maybe for Native academic circles. I guess graduating as many Native students as possible looks pretty good to people in Administration. This teacher now believes the moral of this story is that if you want great marks there, don't do the work and then complain. It's a great time saver. I know Ontario Premier Mike Harris wants to completely restructure the education system but I think this is going a little too far.

Professionalism. A six syllable word that seems to be giving some people a lot of problems. But if my article doesn't appear in the next issue, I still want to be paid.

INDIAN GIVERS

My birthday is approaching quickly and I am beginning to dread it already. Not because Father Time seems to be eating a bigger slice of my birthday cake every year, but because of the presents I might receive from well meaning friends. At the risk of sounding ungrateful, its an interesting comment on society when, as a Native (Ojibway) person, I often receive gifts from my non–Native friends that run the gambit of every possible Native influenced present that could be bought in a store.

For some unexplained reason, there seems to be this subconscious belief amongst many white acquaintances that since I am Native, I must therefore be given a Native–flavoured present at every possible occasion, like a tin logo of the Indian Motorcycle Company that currently hangs on my bedroom wall for example. It seems to be mandatory. To do anything else would be rude and possibly precipitate a blockade of some sort. Thus the clay pottery that I have received over the years that dots my mother's house back home.

In birthday's past, as well as house-warmings, Christmases and a variety of other well known seasonal celebrations, there always seems to be a tendency to give me, as well as many of my Native friends, a confusing collection of Aboriginal giftware. Over the years I alone have received art prints, dreamcatcher's galore, medicine pouches, videotapes of Native movies, and enough t-shirts for a dozen wet t-shirt contests.

For instance, on my last birthday, a good friend of obvious Caucasian ancestry, gave me *Where White Men Fear To Tread*, the autobiography of Russell Means, famed American Indian Movement activist. I appreciated the gesture but it was a rather long book about a man I wasn't particularly interested in knowing better. Being Native doesn't automatically make you interesting. But don't tell him that.

Thus the conundrum. You appreciate the social and financial support for your culture and all it's many artists, but sometimes you just want a pair of black loafers with no feathers attached. I thanked my Caucasian buddy for the gesture anyway.

My former girlfriend took part in the wedding of a longtime friend, she was the only Native participant, and all the bridesmaids and ushers received presents for their efforts. Everybody else in the wedding party received faux diamond jewelry. Instead, my former girlfriend received something called an Answer Feather that consisted of the three staples of First Nations gift giving; a leather strap, a small obliquely carved piece of bone, and a lone feather, quail I believe. According to the tag, it was a "traditional healing tool for those seeking answers," like "why didn't I get any real jewelry?"

Yet on the other hand, my Native friends often give me (and I should add that I often give them) culturally vague clothes, books, appliances, music etc. On many long drives, a CD of Shaggy is just as enjoyable as Kashtin. As I'm writing this, I am wearing a straight black t-shirt with no identifiable Native logo anywhere on it, given to me by a Mohawk family.

If you go to my mother's house on the Reserve, you will notice very little of a representational Aboriginal content in her house. Other than what I give her from the seasonal celebratory overflow that I frequently encounter. In fact, she does have a decidedly non-Aboriginal bar-b-que I gave her for Mother's Day a few years back. And she's as Native as they come. I will confess however, I did give her moccasin slippers one year for Christmas, but only because they were a lot prettier than those worn paisley ones she had. But please don't hate me for that.

It makes me wonder if Native people are not the only recipients of culturally-appropriate tributes. Do Caucasian people feel the urge to give the Japanese chopsticks as a wedding gift? Or maybe Mexicans get sombreros for graduation? Do the Swedish get their national flag at a baby shower? On Arbor Day, do you present your favourite American with an assault rifle? These are difficult questions.

I realize that one shouldn't look a gift horse in the mouth, in fact some may consider it rude and if so I apologize. But I would just like to point out that it is possible to give a gift with no cultural baggage attached. We do manage to exist in other areas of reality besides the Indigenous one. As one friend put it, "there is no particular Native way to boil an egg." The same goes with gift giving.

I look up on my wall, to my Native Images calender, with a good looking Indian guy in a leather vest representing the month of May, and see my birthday not to far distant. I could really use some new dress pants but I better clear a shelf for all the Jack Weatherford and Tony Hillerman novels I know I'll get.

THE WALK THROUGH THE VALLEY OF THE SHADOW OF LITIGATION

Not long ago, my Mohawk girlfriend at the time, came home from the funeral of a relative she was quite fond of. While in the Church, observing the Christian services, she told me she felt uncomfortable. Several times the Minister told the people in attendance to bow their heads in prayer. My girlfriend, instead, choose to look upwards, towards the Creator and think of her uncle in her own way, instead of looking down, away from God, in fear. This was her traditional way of refusing to observe the practices of a belief system she felt had done horrible things to Native people.

Later upon her arrival home, I found myself in the unique position of attempting to defend the Church, though in no way do I call myself a "Christian." I told her not to condemn an entire religion (or several loosely related religions, depending on how you categorize the different Christian faiths) for the acts of a few psychotic pedophiles and culturally blind pseudo-Nazis running the Residential schools. I'm a firm believer that there is some inherent good in all faiths. Churches don't rape children. People rape children. It's just that, in the Native experience, those people who often abused the children, worked for the Church. If you get food poisoning at a McDonald's, you are more likely to blame the company rather than the nineteen year old kid working in the back who didn't wash his hands.

Keeping this in mind, that is not to say the various Churches aren't to blame for their involvement. On the contrary, it's not something they can wash their hands clean of. The age old argument that the head office doesn't know what's going on in the regions will not work in this instance. I see it as being "two

17

degrees of separation" guilt. But as legal precedent would have it, if a man leaves a bar drunk, and then gets into a car accident causing the deaths of someone else, there is legal precedent that the bartender is responsible. I believe that is the case here. Except this time, the accident happened at the Residential school, and the bartender is wearing a cross and parking at the head office.

Right now, there is a battle of blame going on between the Federal Government and the Catholic, Anglican, United, and Presbyterian Churches over legal liability. What's at stake – approximately 7,000 lawsuits against both parties resulting from past abuse and cultural genocide at those same Residential schools. It's like a marriage where the husband and wife are blaming the other for accountability "It's her fault." "No, he's responsible." Settlements could reach into the billions.

The Anglican Church of Canada is already licking its financial wounds and nothing is even close to being settled yet by the courts. Recently, that Church was forced to lay off a dozen employees and drastically cut its budget simply to finance its on–going legal expenses. 1,600 lawsuits can eat up an awful lot of choir uniforms. There is even some discussion of bankruptcy. I bet there's a lot of praying going on at that Church. And justly so.

There is a new law being contemplated by Ontario's Queens Park, dealing with making the parents of youthful offenders financially responsible for damages and fines incurred by their offspring. That seems the perfect law to address the Residential school system situation. Is not the Church often referred to as "Mother Church"? And are we not all seen as the "Children of God"? I know I have personally heard Ministers and Priests use the term "our Heavenly Father." Ergo, our "Heavenly Father" and, lets not forget the equally culpable "Mother Mary," must be at least partially responsible for the actions of the "Children of God." I am no lawyer but I do try to be a logical man.

Perhaps a breach of contract or false advertising suit should also be considered. Most religions offer some form of Heaven or

Paradise for following the beliefs of the Church. But most of the people I have met coming from Residential schools say they were in Hell, and unfortunately, many are still there. I think there's definitely a strong judicial case here.

David Frum, a columnist for the National Post, is quoted as saying he has some difficulty believing that "teaching native children to speak English and adapt to Canadian ways constituted an act of 'cultural genocide'." It is if you're not Canadian and speak a language far older and richer than English, and were here centuries before most columnist's immigrant ancestors got lost trying to find China looking for oregano, paprika and pepper, and ended up bastardizing an Iroquoian word meaning "a small village or group of huts" into a word called Canada which now has a popular ginger ale and beer named after it.

One wonders how he would react if he were placed in a Cree community and beaten every time he spoke English or drank a latte, or went to the cottage or read the Post. I have his bus ticket waiting.

And in reference to learning the English language, I think the operative word Mr. Frum used here is "teaching." "Forcing" might be a better substitute. And as we all know, the conjugation of verbs is best taught through anal penetration. Maybe that's why I failed French in Grade 11.

So maybe its not all that surprising that my girlfriend refuses to pay lip service in a Church. I know my mother still attends Church. As for me... I remember a summer a long time ago when a throng of Pentecostals came to our Reserve. They were there to teach the poor Indians how to play lacrosse (and some religious stuff). After two weeks of mastering the lacrosse stick and ball, they packed up and left. Taking the sticks and balls with them. Leaving behind a group of Native kids who could now play lacrosse but had nothing to play with except a Bible they left behind. Maybe that best explains my view of the Church.

VALENTINE'S DAY

This week, if you're like me, you're aware of two things: first of all, it's St. Valentine's Day – a day of supreme importance to some people, most notably women for some reason; and two, you are desperately trying to figure out what to get a woman who does place some importance on this particular day. And thus, save yourself from getting in a whole whack of trouble instituted by a long dead European saint who has no idea how pissed off a Mohawk girlfriend can get when she doesn't get the right present.

To me, this holiday is like that other holiday with a religious name – St. Patrick's Day. If you're Irish and Catholic, have fun, go nuts. On St. Valentine's Day, if you are Catholic... and I guess like chocolate, go crazy. I am neither so I don't know why I get dragged kicking and screaming into it's fiendish jaws. It's not that I'm not romantic, it's just that limiting your demonstrations of love to just one particular day seems a little sad.

Still, there is that little matter of a present. Do you get her the chocolates, flowers, jewelry, a side of moose, what? All these foreign holidays plays havoc with our First Nations sensibilities. Am I the only one that notices something wrong about the idolization of a fat white man being pulled around the world by a couple of hundred pounds of tasty venison?

In my attempt to become the Dr. Ruth of the Aboriginal set, and answer these complex questions, I have spent days researching libraries, combed the vast recesses of my mind and experiences, searched the forbidden websites on my computer, all in the pursuit of "love" knowledge. I am talking about the experience of passion. The data on amour. The you–know–whats about you–know–what.

I have found that love is many things. And it is not many things. This is not a contradiction. It is called the Zen of Love.

Love is watching Dirty Dancing with your girlfriend 34 times, and constantly acknowledging that "Yes, Patrick Swayze sure is cute. And yes he has a nice body. And he sure can dance really great. And, no dear, I don't know why I can't dance like him." 34 times. And yet she refuses to watch one single boxing match with me. That is love.

They say love means never having to say you're sorry. Well, first of all, "they" never say who "they" are, and I've never been in a relationship where I could get away with not saying "I'm sorry." Again at least 34 times. And God knows I've tried. I've got the scars to prove it. That is not love.

Wanting to buy anything and everything for your woman, to be her Sugar Daddy in other words. But because her family has a history of diabetes, you volunteer to be her Sweet-n'-Low Daddy instead. That is love.

The bottom line: love can be your best friend or your worst enemy it seems. And what a dead Catholic saint knows about loving my girlfriend, I'm sure I'll never know.

STRANGE THINGS

Is it me or has anybody else out there in the Native community noticed two unusual phenomenons that seem to be occurring with increasing frequency? Two actions that, looked at separately, might not seem connected, but put them together... I don't know. I just find it very strange, and disquieting, like aliens have landed. You be the judge.

Unusual activity number one: All the good-looking Aboriginal stud muffins in the performing arts, are cutting their hair. I'm not sure when exactly this started but I think it began around the time Graham Greene got that role in Die Hard 3, a few years back. He got a buzz cut I believe. And from there it's been down hill, folically speaking, for Canada's Aboriginal acting elite.

Darrel Dennis, Adam Beach, Ryan Black, Herbie Barnes, Jonathan Fisher, Dakota House, now all short haired and looking naked. Is it because Kevin Costner's losing his hair? There must be an answer for this sudden lemming-like hair migration. I remember during my days in Native theatre and film, ranging from the mid '80's to just yesterday, and I recollect when the casting room was awash in long haired Indigenous Thespians, trying to launch and sustain their careers, with just a good detangling hair conditioner. Now it looks like they've all joined the army. There's something definitely afoot here.

The other disquieting observation I have made that is taking over the Native community... golf. It has become very apparent to me that in recent years, the game of golf has taken on a rabid fascination to people with a bannock and bingo ancestry. Too many conversations with good friends of mine like Jordan Wheeler and Tom King, are punctuated with golfing metaphors and discussions of handicaps and birdies. It's like a new language. It's frightening when there's no interpreter. What does "a four hundred yard drive on a par four" actually mean to the non-initiated?

In the old days, when somebody came to town for work or a visit, they would usually ask where the nearest Indian bar is or what's the local KFC like? Now the immediate question is for directions to the nearest golf course and what the green fees are. It's become the newest mania. It's the bingo of the new Millennium. Have these people learned nothing from Oka? Do the Warriors of yester-year now swing a five iron and complain about the water hazards? Will they be blockading the twelfth hole?

Oddly enough, there is some sort of Scottish connection to explain this enchantment, since they're the ones who supposedly invented this game. Rumour has it that's also where the original recipe for bannock came from, way back when Scots and Englishmen were paddling up various rivers and lakes looking for fur and Indian women. "Look, we bring you bread and a game where you knock little balls into holes in the ground. Sound like a fair trade?" It would be interesting to get the Aboriginal Feminist perspective on that.

Instead of a Tiger Woods, is there, somewhere on a Reserve located deep in a large sand trap, a young Muskrat Marsh waiting to be discovered? I remember the days when a man said he had a woodie, he was proudly talking about a very bad sexual pun. And when a woman says it, I still do a double take.

So golf and short hair. Is this the future? Is this what the new decade and Millennium have in store for our people? Granted, my hair has always been short and I confess to owning a golf shirt or two. But I refuse to learn the game of golf, just on principle. What's next, cricket and Farrah Fawcett Hairstyles for men maybe?

Be afraid. Be very afraid.

BEING NATIVE DOTH HAVE ITS PRIVILEGES

When I was in college, oh so many years ago, back in the era known as B.C. (Before Computers), I was always trying to make some extra money. One of the ways I found involved working as security in the college pub, all 165 lbs. of me. Much like in porn films, size does matter in jobs of that nature. That's why I always thought I was rather unsuited for an occupation like that and I was mystified by my being hired.

Sometime later, I was told by one of the waitresses who happened to be in one of my classes that somebody higher up the collegiate food chain who was responsible for the Native students had approached the pub manager and pointed out that there had never been a Native person hired to work in the pub. It was also pointed out how "advantageous" it would be to hire me. It was the first time in my life, and I think the only time (summer jobs on the Reserve not included) that I was hired for political and expedient reasons.

Though somewhat upset, I felt like quite the adult – however right or wrong, strings had been pulled in my favour – all for a minimum wage job where nobody liked me. But it also explained why nobody on the staff warmed up to me. Nobody likes somebody who was hired by force, perhaps at the expense of somebody else. I left my momentary career in security after a couple of weeks.

Almost two decades later, I realize just how much things have changed in terms of academic pressure. A close friend of mine teaches Native Studies to a wide variety of students (meaning both Native and non-Native). This person is also currently educating me in the modern usage of flexing Indigenous muscle to get what you want.

It seems where I had people petitioning on my behalf without my knowledge, in today's politically savvy environment, Native students are pulling their strings on their own. And I am truly amazed at what they can get away with, or try to get away with. I say this with the full knowledge that many things can go wrong on the path of education and students must not be afraid to fight for what they believe in. However, I must have missed the class where they taught you how to inflate your cajones and demand better marks for the hell of it.

My friend (who is Native) has had some difficulty recently dealing with two particular Native students who have asked for higher marks than the level they have performed at. One opportunistic student wants full marks for attendance and class participation, even though she missed almost half of the classes, including one to attend a hockey game. And it looks like she might get those extra marks. I definitely went to school in the wrong decade.

And this same student decided one day that she was not going to hand in two course papers simply because she just couldn't get around to doing them. On top of that, the ones she did get around to writing would be submitted a month to two months later. And these students are wondering why their marks are not perfect?

The second student wants her marks raised simply because she didn't like the ones given her, citing the fact she's on academic probation and her funding from the Band might be cut off (which turned out to be incorrect). So rather than earn them, why not just round them up a few extra percentages to make life a lot easier. Other reasons cited include such bizarre rationales as the student having lived a "different life" (who doesn't?) and the marking should reflect and be conscious of it. Wouldn't that make it unfair to those who also had come from "different lives" (what ever the hell that means?) but didn't find the need to use that as a crutch?

So this poses an interesting question. Because somebody is Native, or comes from a Native background, does that mean their standards for success, or the degree of their ability has to be calculated at a lower level than mainstream Canadians? "I am Native – a wolf ate my homework but I still deserve better marks. Give it to me or I'll put a land claim on your student residence!"

During the last thirty or so years, particularly down in the States, there used to be (and still might be for all I know) a quota system for some universities. A certain percentage of enrollment was set aside for Afro-American students, Indian students and what ever other socially oppressed underclass might be apparent.

There was a lot of public outcry from both sides. One side saying that people with marks not up to par with the normal entrance requirements, were merely being promoted because of their race, reverse discrimination and that whole additional argument. Other parties argued it was the only way for the economically and socially disadvantaged populace to compete on an even level with mainstream society. Still more believed it set a lower mark for non–white students to aim for. I tend to believe the latter. But then, I'm not a teacher or a student.

All things taken into consideration... I should have stayed in bar security. Life was more simple there.

BEYOND SKYDOME

It's big. It's noisy. It's flashy as hell. And it's expensive. No, I'm not talking about an ex–girlfriend. I am referring to the Toronto Skydome Pow wow, now known as the Canadian Aboriginal Festival. Think of it as the Indigenous answer to Disneyland. Can you just smell the excitement in the air – no, wait a minute, that's bannock burning. It's a similar aroma.

This is the seventh annual Skydome Pow wow where, in the next two days, it's expected over twenty-five thousand people will grab some corn soup, buy a t-shirt, ask "do those dances and feathers actually mean anything?" and think to themselves, "boy, just look at what paying no taxes on the Reserve can do for you." I guess It's a small price to pay for some venison stew and what looks like to me, the world's largest wigwam. If you don't believe me, compare one to the Skydome yourself.

Now to be fair, there are a lot of people who don't actually like this particular pow wow. They say it's too sophisticated. Too artificial. Too urban I guess. With this hard astroturf beneath our feet instead of Mother Earth, and that huge metal ceiling over our heads instead of Father Sky, it's not what a real pow wow should look or feel like. Kind of like Indian-In-A-Can. And to top it off, that big Jumbotron screen makes everybody look fat. Maybe if we all wear more black beading, I hear it's quite slim-ming... Hmmm...

Twenty–five thousand people. Can you believe it? And most of them not related. Now what kind of real Pow wow is that? But other people might argue the opposite. Skydome Pow wow good! No hot sun, no rain, real bathrooms instead of Johnny-On-The-Spots. The opportunity to go for dim sum after the grand entry. And don't forget, the chance to flare nostrils at that pretty shawl dancer right over the thirty yard line where the Argos lost a football game 52–4. I'm such a romantic at heart.

Personally I like the Skydome Pow wow. Yeah, it's a little more complicated than what our grandfathers may have envisioned. But so is a Jeep Cherokee four by four. What's your point? I mean it's almost December and it's still Pow wow time. Still a chance to dance and enjoy the socializing. And the food... I actually only eat Indian Tacos at pow wows. So technically, this is my last taco of the season. It has to do me until at least May. It better be good.

Last week I was in Alberta, Hobbema to be exact, and I went to my first Rodeo, which was held indoors. I don't think the cowboys of yester-year were anticipating central heating. Or the French fries that were historically sold in Dodge City. True, I do miss the trees and the fresh air of the Reserve setting, nothing will ever take the place of that, but you can't have everything. No blackflies or mosquitoes though. Unfortunately, fresh air and mosquitoes usually go together.

But I guess the real reason all these people are here comes down to a familiar two syllable word – money. Tons and tons of shopping available – one stop shopping for all your Christmas needs.

But an Indian taco costs seven dollars! It cost twelve dollars to get in the doors. If you want a booth here, it will cost you around five hundred dollars, two to three times the cost of any other pow wow. And the prize money... did I mention this was a competition Pow wow? Twenty five thousand dollars for the drummers category and fifty thousand for the best dancers. That's a lot of prime free range baloney, center cut.

I guess Native and white people are not that different.

AMERICA AT WAR

Some people fight wars in very strange ways. On Wednesday, the American government said the horrible devastation in New York and Washington were not acts of terrorism, but acts of war. Judging by the carnage, the brutality, the sheer anonymity of all the victims, I would have to agree. From what I understand, terrorism is usually prompted by a political point, albeit a brutal and often myopic one. But I'll admit the point made by the razing to the ground of the World Trade Centre and the Pentagon was lost on me.

If it is a war, then everything I learned in high school about the history and waging of war was wrong. I was always taught wars were fought over land, resources, and occasionally ideology. Armies against armies. Soldier against soldier. I saw no army in New York or Washington. Only office workers, travel agents, janitors, secretaries, and financial managers. I guess Mr. McLaughlin, my Grade Nine History teacher was wrong.

I am not a historian or a political scientist, but I do know that by it's very nature, war is violence. Death and destruction follow it like eager puppies. However, it's usually a good idea when both sides know there has been a declaration of war I suppose. And if I'm not correct, civilians are suppose to be on the low end of the priority list. But like I said, I don't know that much about war.

America has it's faults. So does Canada for that matter but what I have seen on the television during those incredible past few days makes me wonder about who would wage war in such a horrid manner against unsuspecting and innocent people. It can't be for land or resources. The dangerous and unpredictable world of ideology must be rearing it's ugly head.

Different parts of the world practice war in different ways. The days of Napoleon and Alexander the Great leading their armies into gloriously deconstructed battles are long gone. Nowadays, the people who declare the wars often stay behind, where its safe, and send others to die for them. Some Nations prefer to fight their battles through Guerilla warfare; others through a clear and distinct set of rules.

The Lakota First Nations of the American Plains had their own special rules about engaging the enemy in battle. They had what was called a coup stick, for counting coup. The point was to ride their horse into an opponents camp and hit their enemy with the stick, then ride away. The logic behind that was it didn't take any particular bravery or intelligence to shoot somebody from a safe distance with a gun or arrow.

However, a warrior who could humiliate an enemy, then get away from that still dangerous enemy was truly brave and daring. This was a war of pride, not violence. That whole circling the wagon gun thing developed after contact with European-descended soldiers.

Amongst the Iroquois of the Eastern Woodlands, if a family had lost a son, brother, or husband in battle, it was not uncommon for this same family to adopt a prisoner of war to replace them. I guess this is a different way of waging war. On a tactical scale, no doubt less effective in the long run than flying jets into buildings. But still, a rose is a rose is a rose...

I guess all this splitting hairs matters little to those who didn't survive these acts of war and their families. Once the shock and numbness wears off the real impact of September 11th, will hit. It's the first war fought in the continental United States, excluding the Indian Wars, since the Civil war ended in 1865.

CASTING AN INDIGENOUS BALLOT

The topic on most Aboriginal minds these days? To vote, or not to vote. That is the question. Whether tis nobler, or more politically expedient to join the rest of Canada in trying to figure out which of the party leaders is the lesser of evils, or perhaps just ignore the whole thing and go bowling instead. A tough question indeed.

Some have argued that, maybe, as Native people we should just sit this and all other elections out. Because participating in the Canadian electoral process might compromise our status as independent First Nations. Canada made its treaties with sovereign autonomous Aboriginal Nations and we shouldn't participate in their government anymore than they have a right to participate in ours. We are not Canadians. We are "insert your Nation here."

Personally, I don't think it's as cut and dry as that. Granted there is a reasonable amount of logic to the argument but on the other hand, I've met too many Native war veterans who fought for and lost friends defending Canada. I'd feel uncomfortable telling them they didn't have the right to vote.

On a completely different hand, I've been to Church a handful of times but I don't consider myself Christian. I've eaten a lot of Chinese food but I'm fairly certain I'm not Chinese (Szechuan or Cantonese). When I swim, I dog paddle. I don't think that makes me a poodle. Politics, like many things in life, is not always "all or nothing." I think you're allowed to fudge the boundary lines occasionally.

Don't get me wrong, I am not suggesting by any means that you should rush out and vote into office your favourite older white person who's probably a lawyer to boot. I'm not sure if I'll

31

vote. Nobody's even talking about Native issues during this election which makes it all the more difficult to decide.

I mean, look at the parties and what they have to propose: The Liberals are offering all sorts of yummy tax breaks. You can never go wrong appealing to a Nation' wallet. Of course, a sizable percentage of Native people are tax exempt (or live below the poverty line and wouldn't have to pay taxes anyways), so I'm not sure how important that is to us.

There's also that saving the Health Care system thing they are bragging about constantly. With the amount of diabetes and other ailments common to the Native community, that is certainly a factor to keep in mind.

Then there's the Bloc Quebecois? Who? Actually, I have sources that have told me, if you can believe it, that there are actually seven Aboriginal people who plan to vote for the B.Q. But they live in Alberta so it's not really an issue.

The New Democrats have always been supportive of Native causes. Tax the rich – how many rich Indians do you know? Sounds great. But with all the social programs they envision, this would necessitate a bigger bureaucracy and government, which I know for a fact would send a chill down many an Aboriginal's back. Based on our past experiences, asking for a bigger government would be like asking for a bigger Residential school.

And it's no secret where the Alliance Party stands on Native issues. They want to eliminate all special status for us Indigenous people, and make us like everybody else. That includes the implementation of taxation, elimination of Reserves and the selling of Reserve land (turning communal property into private property). That's mighty white of them, don't you think? This was tried thirty years ago by the Liberals with their infamous White Paper which in turn caused one of the last great Indian uprisings.

I guess the best way to simply explain Indigenous rights the Alliance Party is to talk in their language of big business. And I can explain it in one word. Seniority. I'm sure they're familiar with that concept. Basically, that means those that have been with the company the longest, and put in the most time, get promoted and bigger pay cheques. A time honoured business tradition.

Using that philosophy, it isn't that difficult to understand the Native people of this country having seniority over everybody else. We have certainly put in the time and effort into this corporation known as Canada/Turtle Island. Quite a bit of seniority in fact. Hell, I've been waiting for my promotion for years.

I guess it's safe to say the Alliance Party is hoping Canadians will see the White of day... sorry, that's suppose to be the light of day. Light of Day (as in Stockwell Day). How could I make that mistake?

And speaking as an artist, he once supported the banning of funding for books and wants to eliminate grants to artists and privatize the CBC. Hey, I have a hungry mortgage to feed and a mother to keep in pasta. But if he has his way, before you know it, the CBC's motto will be "All Gilligan, all the time!"

As for what's left of the Tory party? These days, finding an actual party member is more difficult than finding a Beothuk. The only good thing they have on their side is the fact that in 1960, the Conservatives were responsible for giving Native people the vote. I bet you didn't know nostalgia and good Karma could last forty years.

So come election day... what am I gonna do? What are you gonna do? Does anybody really care? Maybe I'll stay home or perhaps I'll vote for that Marxist party I hear about. I've always loved their movies.

THE CHANGING OF THE GUARD

What a month! Stockwell Day of the Alliance Party and Matthew Coon Comb of the Quebec Cree Party all elected to office after a stunning upset over their predecessor. Democracy – thy name is fickle. Pretty soon Day, still smelling of Alberta cattle and Coon Comb, reeking of Quebec Tamarac, will be moving to Ottawa to take up residence and begin governing their individual feifdoms. The Chief is dead – Long live the Chief. Maybe the two of them can car pool or something. Now that would make for some pretty interesting travel conversations.

Now admittedly, I'm not exactly up on my right wing, conservative, religious, white people – which is a shame considering we should know better after the last five hundred years. So I'm a little vague on what Day could mean to your average brown skinned Indigenous inhabitant. However I am aware that the original Reform Party was not too Aboriginally–friendly in many of their policies. But as the old saying goes, never judge a bannock before it's fried.

But I do have a few friends working in the head office of the Assembly of First Nations in Ottawa and the main topic of conversation involves wondering if they'll have a job next month. And that's one of the things I find so admirable in that organization – the sense of tradition they freely practice.

I am talking about the age old practice that begins when a new Reserve Chief is elected, deposing another. You can practically set your watch by the exodus of the past Chief's entourage (friends, family, girlfriends) who all worked in the Band Office. And the flood of new friends, family and girlfriends (or in these politically correct times, boyfriends and possibly small farm animals too) as they pour into the Administration Office to claim their cubicle.

So I guess all of Phil Fontaine's people will be snapping up most of those juicy heavy equipment operator and bingo calling jobs.

Typically, in most communities, I've heard that a quarter of the yearly budget will be spent in ordering new business cards, letterhead, name plates for doors and desks, and stocking up on that Swiss Mocha coffee the new Chief is so fond of.

Of course I'm not sure if Matthew Coon Comb is a Swiss mocha fan, or maybe he's just an old fashioned tea drinker from those days on the trapline with his father. I'm told it's hard to take an espresso machine into the bush.

So with all these things happening in the wilds of distant Ottawa, I'm curious to find out what this means to the average individual Indian. Probably not much. Storms at the top of the mountain rarely can be felt in the valleys. And because, for so long, most decisions were made on our behalf by people we never saw or met. So I think there is an unfortunate tendency in many grassroots Aboriginals to shrug off politics on a grander scale. If it weren't for the fact that I occasionally find myself in political situations, working with political people (I used to date a socialist but she discovered that I made too much money and we had to break up), and sometimes writing about such things, I would probably be thinking Coon Comb was a new breakfast cereal.

A Vice–Chief once criticized me for not spending more time writing about important issues that were more pertinent to our people. "Like What? I inquired. "Like Nationhood" he responded. That week I think I was working on an article on Native Erotica. I asked several of my friends which were they most likely to read, an article on Native Erotica or one on Aboriginal Nationhood. I don't think I have to tell you the answer.

Several years ago, during both the Meech Lake Accord fiasco and the Charlottetown Accord debacle, I would frequently find myself being asked "what the hell is this all about?" when ever I returned home to my Reserve. For some silly reason, it was assumed I was in the "know." But luckily I would have

35

some vague idea of what was going on and could give a twenty second synopsis as seen through the eyes of somebody that just recently heard the Vietnam War was over. Next on my agenda is to find out who won it. My money is on the Koreans.

So, Mr. Coon Comb, enjoy your new life as the voice of the people. I'm sure you will do wonders for our people. The buzz around the Aboriginal water cooler is very favourable. Besides, you look good in a suit.

Maybe the next time I'm in town, we can do lunch. Of course, the cheque will be on you because I heard a rumour that you're called the "Grand" Chief because that's your weekly take home pay. That will buy an awful lot of Swiss mocha.

And if you have the chance, buy Stockwell Day a coffee. Be nice to him. He too is new in town.

GETTING TRASHED

It seems that practically everywhere you go in Canada, some-body has issues with the City of Toronto. For a place with a good Aboriginal name, you'd think people would like it. But occa-sionally, the city does something to warrant that attitude. There is now yet another town, a Reserve actually, with another Native name that has joined the Toronto hating community with a vengeance. I am talking about the Timiskaming First Nations, located in Northern Ontario.

It seems that Toronto, in it's need to dispose of the garbage of three million people, came dangerously close to dumping their refuse in the backyard of this innocent little Ojibway com-munity. The good people of Timiskaming and Kirkland Lake huffed and puffed but to no good. Toronto was determined to ship the equivalent of 250 truckloads a day of rotting Chinese food, pizza boxes, and used q-tips to fill an abandoned strip mine, doing God knows what to the local environment. Charming image, huh?

The Chief and community of Timiskaming vowed to do bat-tle against Toronto to prevent this rubbish invasion, threatening to make Oka look like a bar-b-que. In the end, it was a small technical clause in a contract that ended up sinking the garbage ship. A clause having nothing to do with Timiskaming but instead, dealing with a matter of who would pay for cost over-runs.

Even deep in the heart of Toronto, you could hear the sigh of relief coming from Timiskaming. But personally, I don't know what all the fuss was about. I mean, it would have given the residents of Timiskaming the opportunity to do what white anthropologists have been doing for years – rooting through somebody else's garbage. And believe it or not, these people get paid for it. For some weird reason, these scientists get all hot and bothered when they find a six hundred year old trash heap than when their wives come home from a lingerie party.

Now I've been to a Native garbage dump and to tell you the truth, I really don't know what the thrill is. The most exciting thing I ever found there were six coffee stained superman comic books. It wasn't much but to my mind, it sure beat the hell out of a broken arrowhead. Maybe its an Aboriginal thing.

So I was thinking, let's be clever about this garbage thing. If a post–graduate student can get a PhD and then tenure at a major university by analyzing a thousand year old soup bone, the mind boggles at what the Timiskaming people could have done with old credit card receipts, love letters and discarded computer disks.

Where some people see a potential environmental disaster, I see opportunity. So I came up with an easy solution should the people of Timiskaming need one in the future. At most archeological excavations, everything is dug up and then shipped off to a museum for study.

So late some night, they should sneak into the garbage dump, sprinkle a thin layer of dirt over it, and throw down some broken arrowheads. Hell, you can get those in any store cheap. Go to the band office petty cash, get a quarter, make an anonymous call to a local university... and I can practically guarantee you that place will be dug up so quickly and shipped off to a museum before you can shout land claim.

It's all in how you approach a problem and comprehend how the white mind works. Next week, my solution to the Ozone problem using the Alliance Party hot air.

ABORIGINAL HOROSCOPE

ARIES
Good news! This is your month. I hope you can afford the payments. The stars will truly shine on you for the next four weeks until you get the roof repaired. Enjoy life. Be confident. Grab the tiger by the tail, unless you are at the zoo.

TAURUS
This is the month for love. Taurus, be prepared to be swept off your feet because chances are, he or she will be a janitor. Play hard to get before he gets to be hard. Love can be fickle, so don't be afraid of disappointment. That's why God created gas cans and lighters.

GEMINI
Wear clean underwear. Floss your teeth. Never tip more than 15%. Call home more often. Get a "real" job. Get a hair cut. Don't act so silly. Slow down, you drive too fast. You call that bannock!? Try to lose some weight. So, who are you seeing now? Your mother will play a more active role in your life this month.

CANCER
Don't forget to pee this month.

LEO
Ominous signs are everywhere. Beware of all one-legged men who stutter when they sing Aztec operas. They are everywhere. Caution and prudence should guide you during this fateful month – I am of course referring to Caution and Prudence Kakagamic, two guides at the hunting camp I go to.

VIRGO

Be careful how you spend your money. You might be suscepti-
ble to impulse buying. So do not buy more than one Ford
Impulse car during this period. This is also a time for important
and urgent decisions, so Band counselors beware, this is not
your month. Wear more plaid.

LIBRA

Children will play an important part in your life. Hopefully they
will be yours. This would be the perfect time to work on your
parenting skills. Remember, change diapers on baby more frequently than you water the plants. Or let them run free in the
backyard, unadorned, as nature intended.

SCORPIO

This is an opportune time to settle all outstanding land claims
and institute any new policies. From now on, any real estate or
land sold to non–Native people will be strictly by the kilogram.
Don't be afraid to have an "All You Can Carry Sale."

SAGITTARIUS

Spring is here and it's time to get a new wardrobe. Or at least a
new pair of rubber boots. Get rid of all your old clothes and greet
the new season in style – naked. Enjoy the feeling of revitaliza-
tion and renewal because from here on out, it's downhill for you.

CAPRICORN

Things do not look good for Capricorn's this month. Make sure
you are insured. Don't forget to say the appropriate good-byes.
Remember to make out a will. Or make out with anybody named
Will. And if Will is a lawyer, do both. If you owe money, don't
bother paying it back – if they want their money bad enough, let
them follow you and get it. Your lucky number for this month,
911.

AQUARIUS
Take a Cree to lunch. If it's a full moon, have the pasta special.

PISCES
The 15th till the 18th will be your lucky days. Expect a run on pregnancy kits at the local stores soon after. Stay away from bingos but don't be afraid to try your luck at the casinos. With any luck, chance will play a very big part in your life this month. Pisces should also look to their sign animal, the mighty salmon, for guidance. Except for that "floating belly up and really dead once the journey has finished" thing.

SOME OF MY BEST FRIENDS ARE VEGETABLES

There's an old joke in the Native community that goes something like "What's another term for an Indian vegetarian?" The
appropriate answer: "A very bad hunter."

Finding a Native vegetarian is something akin to finding a
non-bingo going, non-hockey watching/playing, non-denim
wearing, non–dreamcatcher/feather-hanging-from-the-rear-
view mirror type Indigenous person. But for some reason, there
seems to be whole masses of non-Native ones out there, in
Canadian society, drinking their carrot juices and eating muffins
galore, sending dirty looks at us carnivores (whether Indigenous
or not). I think there must be a scientific lab somewhere spitting
these people out.

Now I'm not a vindictive or petty person, but in my travels
I have met many people who have pet peeves, or groups of people that annoy or irritate other assortments of people. I am no
different. Over the years and after many a tasty veal sandwich,
it has been my dubious pleasure to face many a renegade vegetarian who have strong, definite opinions about my diet and
aren't afraid to express it to my face. For the record, I am a proud
meat eater. I keep a pepperoni in my wallet for emergencies.
When I die, I don't want to be cremated, instead I want to be
marinated and bar-b-qued. And unfortunately I have many an
ex-girlfriend who would volunteer for the job. And some who
wouldn't necessarily wait for me to die before starting.

In fact, an example of my devotion to DNA consumption
can be observed in the oddest places, like during my occasional
bouts of tequila festivities. Instead of doing the normal sequen-
tial routine of salt, tequila, and then a lemon to cleanse the
palate, I instead opt for the more interesting salt, tequila, then a

pork chop. Unconventional but definitely more tasty I think, not to mention the benefits of the additional protein.

Upon seeing this, one vegetarian woman I met told me that, on principle, she refuses to eat anything with a face. Poor woman, I couldn't help thinking, she must be terrible in bed! But then again, I guess nothing beats a good carrot.

Personally, I think this vegetarian/carnivore rivalry goes all the way back to Biblical times. It's all right there in the Bible, if you know how to read between the lines. Check out the first few books of Genesis. As you may remember, Adam and Eve are hanging around the Garden of Eden, looking for ways to screw up Paradise (you may know their great-great-great-great grandson, a gentleman named Columbus).

So there's our innocent Eve, with nothing much to do, hanging around this strange and unusual tree with a name plate nailed into the bark saying "Do Not Touch". She looks up and sees something in the tree, reminding her that she was hungry. So what does she pick from it that gets her, her hubby, and all their descendants tossed by God from the Garden of Eden and thrust forever into the Hell we now know as Urban Sprawl?

If my bible studies are correct, I believe it was the proverbial "forbidden FRUIT." The operative word here is fruit! Not steak, not roast chicken, not even a lamb chop, but fruit! My question is, would all the troubles of the world have happened, would civilization be different if, say, instead she had picked some veal piccata? Or maybe we'd still be running around naked and happy if she'd had a craving for some chicken wings. Would we still be in Paradise if she had passed on the fruit for a beef and broccoli stir fry? It does make a person wonder. Mental note: I must remember to send a copy of this column to the Pope. Could be some interesting theological discussions here.

So instead, all these thousands of years later, I get my jollies by telling vegetarians that we Native people consider pet stores on the same par with take out Restaurants. The number of times I've told someone I was going by the Pets'R'Us to pick up some rabbits and then innocently asked, "Anybody want me to grab them some fish or maybe a kitten or two as an appetizer?" I mean, if you just hollow out the kitten from the top, they make dandy slippers, depending on your shoe size. For some reason, vegetarians don't appreciate my sense of humour.

Oh well, one thing I know for sure. When the end of the world finally does come, whether it's the next ice age or maybe global warming, I'm fairly certain it will be us big and fat meat eaters who'll end up eating the thinner, anemic vegetarians. Survival of the fattest. The good thing is, at least they'll be low-fat!

WHAT IF MORE THAN SANTA'S SUIT WAS RED?

Every once in a while, the fabulous and endless world of the internet coughs up something interesting. For instance, just the other day, I received an email from a friend detailing the top ten things that would be different if Santa were an Indian/ Aboriginal/ Indigenous/ First Nations/ Native (pick one of the above). In the spirit of the Yuletide season, I offer this list out to you as a Christmas present, somewhat rewritten, lengthened and Canadianized!:

15. Santa is actually a Mohawk doing aerial surveillance for the Warrior Society.

14. All the American Reservations going without presents: Stop for American beer and cigarettes? "I don't think so!" says Santa.

13. Deer dropping left at all A.A. meeting halls/ diabetes clinics/ bingo parlors/ homes of all blonde women (pick any of the above).

12. Last minute delay in the delivery of presents as all mail addressed to the North Pole diverted to Nunavut.

11. At bedtime, kids would leave corn soup and fry bread/ scone/bannock/cornbread (pick one of the above) for the big guy.

10. Most of his reindeer would be called "you stupid animal!"

9.   Santa's new moccasins are made out of Dasher.

8.   There's a new air claim on all the routes Santa has been using since Time Immemorial.

7.   Five pounds of cheese/bread/flour/government meat (pick one of the above) under every tree.

6.   His elves would never show up for work on Fridays and sometimes Mondays.

5.   Santa would have to add two extra deer to help get his belly off the ground.

4.   The sleigh would need a boost every other Province.

3.   His outfit would consist of a red flannel ribbon shirt, with matching leggings, moccasins and beaded black belt with matching beaded rimmed hat, all to match his oversized beaded gift bag. And underneath would be a beaded thong with a small delicate plume attached to the back.

2.   Indian preference would require you to hire the Salish to fit in those teeny tiny elf outfits.

And the number one way things would be different if Santa were a skin...?

1.   According to Indian time, our gifts would arrive in February.

But realistically, Santa could never be an Indian. Do you really think twenty million white people would allow an Indian to break into their homes at will?

INDIAN HUMOUR – WHAT A JOKE!

I was recently in Winnipeg where I learned an important lesson dealing with the ticklish issue of humour, or what some people think is humour.

I had arrived late for dinner with a group of journalists from the APTN network where I had just appeared on a talk show dealing with Aboriginal humour. I sat in the only available chair, beside a man I had been introduced to earlier in the day, and two young women I had not yet met. No sooner had I sat down when the guy beside me yelled to the two women in front of me "Hey, this is Drew Hayden Taylor and he's promised to give you each a screaming orgasm. And wait'till you hear him scream!" That was my introduction to these women. For one of the few times in my life, I was speechless.

For the rest of the evening, he peppered the table with a non–stop barrage of jokes, most of which I'm fairly certain, only he found funny. The evening ended with a series (I'm talking at least a good ten minutes worth) of constant Ojibway jokes aimed directly at me. Now I can take a joke as good as the next person, even more so since as a "professional" humourist (though some might argue), I have studied and experienced a lot of wit in the world. One would think I should have a higher tolerance for the more abstract forms of joking. I was wrong.

This man's constant attempts at being funny kept reminding me of boxing statistics, when the ringside announcers say that a particular boxer threw 112 punches in a round but only 13 were power shots. It was roughly the same ratio. And typically, the more he drank, the funnier he thought he was... sound vaguely familiar? At the end of the evening, the man's superior at work came up to me and apologized for the guy's behavior. I shrugged

47

off the effect of the man's impact on me, thinking they had to deal with him more than I did. I was leaving the next day.

As everyone knows, comedy is subjective. Everybody has a different funny bone. Some laugh at the Three Stooges, others at Married With Children, and there's Shakespeare, and lets not forget the limited appeal of Mimes. Truly, I have yet to meet anybody (who is not a Mime) who will actually admit to enjoying and understanding the profession. Though the one universal element in the universe, after death and taxes (of which we as Native people had more of one and less of the other) is everybody knows somebody who thinks they are funnier than they actually are. Someday they'll have a way of screening the DNA to prevent this.

In researching and editing a documentary I directed on Native humour for the National Film Board, I was privileged to explore and ascertain the wonderfully full and amazing forms of Aboriginal humour existing in this country, specifically the distinctive characteristics or aspects that seem to appear more in our humour than in other cultures (screaming orgasms not withstanding). And you don't have to be a "professional" humourist to figure this out.

For instance, teasing seems to be the predominate form of witty banter amongst our people. Everybody has been teased by a child, adult or peer. You ain't Indian if you can't tease or be teased – it's mentioned somewhere in the Royal Commission on Aboriginal People, Section 4.3.6: "The Federal Government will acknowledge the right of Aboriginal people in this country to tease, be teased, as well as hunt and fish and all the rest of it". IN some Aboriginal cultures, it is a specific mechanism used in the society to keep people in line and maintain the status quo, the great social adjuster.

Also, our humour tends to be quite self-deprecating. That is to say, we tend to make jokes about ourselves, often at our own expense. How many people out there have told an "Indian" joke or made fun of themselves, family or friends? It seems quite natural. Again, it's also a way of maintaining social unity and keeping our feet on the ground.

Another unusual attribute deals with the ability to start a joke, and have it carry on, with various individuals building and adding on to it until a completely different joke finally emerges. Sitting around a table or fire, somebody tells a joke or teases somebody, and another person adds on to it until it lands in somebody else's lap. A soundly Indigenous practice I believe.

It's important to point out that these characteristics are not just limited to the Native community. There are exceptions to every rule. I for one, have seen many white people tease each other, and the mainstay of many Jewish comedians is the self-deprecating joke. However, I think over the thousands of years, we have created and mastered our own unique brand of it.

Some words of advice to wannabe funny-people out there. As somebody who's told a lot of jokes in his day and had a few of them fall flat, and also seen many people tells jokes that were funny and not funny, take notice of some experienced suggestions on tickling the funny bone, whether Indigenous or not.

Rule # 1 – The moment you try to be funny, is the moment you sound like you're trying to be funny. It's got to be natural and spontaneous (which defines the vast majority of Native people I know). You shouldn't have to push or force your jokes into people's faces.

Rule # 2 – Humour should amuse, not abuse. Most people tell jokes to entertain or obtain friends. Abusing them does not help you in your cause. I must remember to email that message to Winnipeg.

And I am tempted to urge people not to laugh at their own jokes, but there is another unique quality about some Native humour I forgot to mention. In some communities, particularly up north, you don't know you're being teased until they themselves start laughing. This is because the humour is so subtle and understated. I learned that the hard way.

And stay away from jokes about screaming orgasms unless you know the person.

And for the record, I don't scream.

WHAT'S A SELF RESPECTING INDIAN TO DO?

In this complex world of Aboriginal issues and Native politics, it's sometimes kind of hard for your basic grass-roots person of Indigenous descent, such as myself, to make heads or tails of what he or she should do in the volatile bureaucratic world we live in. Or in layman's terms, what do you do when you want to be a good little Indian and support the cause, or causes, without causing a political faux pas.

Back in the days of Oka, it was a lot easier to make a statement against the hated "Establishment." You wanted to support the people at Kanehsatake in their fight against an evil, encroaching golf course of the dominant white capitalism that still threatens to engulf the world. Or something like that. So to stop the encroaching demons of Hell, you refuse to learn, play or take up the game of golf, out of principle. Those little white balls become diabolic. Anything above the ninth hole becomes purgatory. All good Native people had huge golf bag bonfires kindled with scorecards. Only the blasphemous still swing a nine iron.

It seemed pretty cut and dry. But in more recent years, making a political statement to support your brothers and sisters has become a little more difficult, at least for yours truly. With the protests over the Temagami and Lubicon Lake forestry/pulp paper issue, things became a little more shadowy for Native people who do what I do.

As a writer, even in this electronic age, it's hard to walk away from the paper industry. That's what most of my articles and plays end up being printed on. You're probably reading this right now on paper. I get paid in cheques which are printed on paper, or sometimes in money, also printed on paper.

Even worse on the paper necessity scale, I still remember my childhood, the visits to the outhouse, having to make do with an Eaton's catalogue. I now wake up screaming with visions of my books ending up waiting their turn in a two holer due to a paper shortage... Still, you want to be supportive, somehow.

And with all the events happening in Burnt Church, New Brunswick, it makes things a bit stickier. Deep inside, my Aboriginal heart cries out to support our Micmac brethren. Every day I find myself fighting the impulse to rush out to my local seafood shop and buy a dozen lobster for the cause, lobsters wearing cute little camouflage outfits so you know they're the real thing. My little way of waging economic war and providing financial support. Except for one minor little detail. I hate lobster. I really can't stand the creatures. It's like eating a water spider with an over-active pituitary gland.

So it makes me wonder, am I letting my compatriots down, or should I force those creepy looking things with big claws down my throat, regardless of the consequences? Sometimes the cost of political support can truly be frightening.

So, in the end, taking everything into consideration, am I a failure? I don't golf. I should get browny points for that one. But unfortunately I still buy paper, to write on, to read, and while I don't frequent as many outhouses as I once did as a youth, I accomplish the same task using a different type of paper. And as for the lobster... sorry, not for all the Micmacs in the world.

I guess I am a failure, two strikes out of three. I am not a good Indian. Maybe I will take up golf then. The idea of hitting little white balls with something metal kind of appeals to me in a weird sort of way.

I hope I'm not barred from the next pow wow.

GETTING THE N.A.C*
(*Native Artistic Community)

WHERE'D THAT ARROW IN MY BACK COME FROM?

There are three things in this world I would urge people, if they have any sanity, never to be or do. The first two are unimportant but the third definitely would include the dubious endeavor of being a critic or reviewer in the Native artistic community. Because no matter what you may write, you can be sure somebody you know will not like it and make sure that you know they do not like it. Or they will never talk to you again.

It is undoubtedly one of the advantages of coming from a larger, dominant culture when you can say or write what you want about other people's work, and conceivably never have to worry about running into these people and face the proverbial music (unless of course you're a proverbial music critic).

Not so in the Native community. In Canada, the Native population is fairly small. The Native artistic community is even smaller. And in a place like Toronto, most would fit in my mother's back yard for a bar-b-que. As a playwright, I know almost all the other Aboriginal playwrights in Canada, as well as the vast majority the actors and directors. As a published author, I also know most of the other First Nations writers on a personal level. As a Native filmmaker... you get the picture.

And with the advent of political correctness, its no surprise that many institutions that review books, plays, films etc. would prefer to avoid the hassle of seeming insensitive to the artistic aspirations of this country's Indigenous population, and at the same time, review their work without a potentially "racist" slant. So often times, they call on a First Nations peer. That's where I often enter the picture, like a lamb to slaughter.

Everybody has an opinion. Some people have too many

opinions. And in this insane world we live in, a very few people are paid for their opinion. These people are called critics and they make a few bucks sharing their opinion of other people's work. These are often, though not always, people who don't actually participate in the art they comment on.

So I think it's important to point out that unlike many critics, I actually work in the fields I may review. Otherwise, what's the point of offering up an uneducated opinion. God knows there's enough of those in the world already. Critics can sometimes be like people who watch a lot of porn but never have sex. More akin to do as I say, not as I do.

In the past I have reviewed books by Tom King, Brian Maracle, Richard Wagamese etc. movies ranging from Dances with Wolves to Pocahontas, written my opinion about various television shows, and many detailed articles on exploring and explaining the world of Aboriginal theatre. So needless to say, I've pissed off a lot of people. And as I have stated, eventually you will run into these same people at a Starbucks, a pow wow, or a book launching.

Some critics have the luxury of divorcing themselves completely from the people they write about. Because of the vastness of the non–Native art world, this is more than possible, even preferable. But as a participating member of both the artistic community and the Native community, that is not a conceivable option for me.

And the ironic thing is, I'm not an exceptionally brutal critic, I sometimes bend over backwards trying to find positive things to say about the material I am reviewing. And as a result, I have turned down more assignments than I have taken to avoid any unnecessary awkwardness or possible unpleasantness.

This is because, in the Native community, there is often perceived to be a fine line between those who support our artists, and those who feel the need to be critical and drag them down. It's often referred to in an over-used cliché known as "the crab story."

It goes something like this: A man was walking down the beach one day and saw this Native man approaching. In the Native man's hand was a pail. Inside the pail was a bunch of live crabs. The man commented to the Native man "You better put a lid on your pail or all your crabs will get away." The Native man shook his head with a smile, saying "I don't need a lid. They're Indian crabs, the minute one of them makes it to the top, the others will pull him back down."

That is often the danger of writing from inside a marginalized group. I have been told numerous times: "After five hundred years of oppression and suppression, what our nations need is positive reinforcement and encouragement. Otherwise, you're playing into their hands, and dividing us in our time of cultural Renaissance. We must stand together and support our brothers and sisters in their endeavors."... or something like that.

As a result, the objectivity in reviews can be a little suspect. In many of the Native magazines I have read or seen in my professional life, the review section consisted of 99.9% glowing praise if the book/film/album was Native-originated. It got to the point where if I saw the word REVIEWS, I didn't bother reading the text because I knew instinctively it would be kind words and rabid support. Again, it's difficult to consider such support a fault after several hundred years of being told our stories and arts were worthless and meaningless. Thus the conflicted nature of being a Native critic.

I've been told this issue is not unique to specifically the Native community. Many have told me that such divided opinions on the merits of accurate and informed criticism have rallied opposing sides of many marginalized communities i.e. the Gay and Lesbian community, the Asian, Jewish, Black, French-Canadian, Left-handed walnut merchants etc. It is perceived that an objective opinion can quickly be misconstrued as a personal attack and the reviewer has been corrupted by main-stream sensibilities.

In my artistic community where the playwright population may consist of a dozen or two, every time you say/write something like "So'n'So's dialogue seemed a little cliched and could have been a tad more original," it's not anonymous words from an anonymous patron. Especially when you've sat at the bar with this fellow writer, lent them money, called them a cab, or they've called you a cab, then it seems like a betrayal, regardless of the accuracy of your comments. I personally have received long letters deconstructing my reviews and pointing out, both rudely and politely, how invalid my opinion is. And that's what a review is, simply an opinion.

And as somebody who has received more than his share of criticism in the arts, some positive, some negative, I truly understand the value of accurate and insightful criticism. Many of my non–artistic friends have often said that they envied me and wished they could be a critic, be paid to read books or watch movies, or listen to music. Most don't understand that to be a movie critic, you need more than the ability to eat popcorn and say "I like it" or "I don't like it."

I've told them that if you like something, you have to be able to tell them why you liked it, concisely and intelligently. What stood out, what grabbed your nuts (or ovaries) and squeezed them until you felt something? Or on the other hand, "That movie sucked" doesn't exactly inspire confidence in the reviewer's capacity to eloquently present their case.

One of the reasons I don't review a lot of books or movies is I hate the detached feeling you must have in order to write about it – the ability to analyze while participating. Not something I find easy or enjoyable to do. And you'll find it's often easier to say why you disliked something rather than why you liked it, because the things that disturb or confuse you, are more obvious and easier to put your thumb on.

So with all that being said, reviewing somebody's work is a huge responsibility. Reviewing somebody's work in the Native community, is fraught with delicate considerations and potential social misunderstandings. However, growth comes from constructive criticism, be it Native or non-Native. Art, like reality and life, will have its detractors and benefactors. The real trick is to take what you can, and ignore the rest. Easier said than done, but it sure beats getting an ulcer, or an arrow in the back.

57 CHANNELS AND NO INDIANS ON

My suspicions as to the status of Canadian television, and to a lesser extent American television, were realized when I received a phone call while waiting in the Lethbridge airport to board a flight to Saskatoon. It was a call that couldn't have come at a better time.

To start off with, I was troubled and depressed. I'd spent almost the last two years trying to develop a Native sketch comedy show *a la' In Living Colour* for the CBC, and like a poorly executed first date, the CBC said "not interested" and told me to take "Seeing Red" and go home.

The best metaphor (or simile) I can come up with for the process of series development is it's like white-water canoeing, except you're going against the current. Without a canoe.

Canadian television had once welcomed the Aboriginal perspective with open arms. For its nineteen year run, usually a third of the cast of *The Beachcombers* were Native, and then more recently there was *Spirit Bay*, *North Of Sixty* and *The Rez* all which broke new ground and let Canadians see how Native people function in this country. Today, as the summer sun of 2001 burns us all red, everyone of these shows are buried in a collective grave, somewhere in the dark and dank cemetery known as the CBC archives or the Happy Haunting Grounds as we Natives call it.

Dead Dog Cafe, a brilliantly satirical radio show written by Cherokee/Greek novelist Tom King, kept CBC radio listeners amused for five years before voluntarily going off the air this year. "After writing eighty-five scripts, you sort of run out of gas after doing the same thing for so long. Luckily I hadn't run out yet but I didn't know how much more I had" explained Tom

King. "At heart I am a novelist and [the show] prevented me from writing novels. Radio shows have deadlines, novels don't. It was time to kill the dead dog."

Though, according to CBC big wig George Anthony, reports of the shows death may be greatly exaggerated. Like a new *Star Trek* series, it may refuse to stay in the grave. "We're currently assessing at least three separate proposals to bring the CBC Radio hit *"DEAD DOG CAFE"* to CBC Television, including a fairly ambitious animated version." But like many a weary television writer has found, the road to series riches is often fraught with network executives.

But tonight sitting on the couch, what Indigenous representations does that leave us on Canadian television... supporting characters on *Blackfly* and the Evening News – the conclusion being the bloom is off the rose. Ojibway actor Herbie Barnes believes the fading interest was to be expected. "I think it's a natural progression. They found something new and it's not new anymore. That is the nature of television."

Movies too. It wasn't all that long ago when theatrical and television movies were being produced all over Canada that explored the Native reality; *Dance Me Outside, Where The Spirit Lives, Clearcut, Blackrobe, Spirit Rider,* and the most recent being *Big Bear,* to name just a few.

Carol Greyeyes, former Artistic Director of the Centre for Indigenous Theatre, blames our invisible status on television and film producers. "And when you think about it, it's not really their job [to portray Native people accurately]. Basically they're there to make money and if Native people happen to be the flavour of the month, then they'll exploit that. And Native People are no longer lucrative, or Hollywood and the networks have gone "oh, the trend is over. Let's move on to something else." Last year, if memory serves me correctly, necrophiliacs were the big ticket item in Canadian cinema.

When I traveled the globe, I was always proud to tell the world that Canada was at least a decade or two ahead of the Americans in the representation of Native people in the media.

Over the years, some American shows occasionally donated at least a token episode or two to Aboriginal causes – *Seinfeld*, *Barney Miller*, *X-Files*, *The Brady Bunch*, *The Partridge Family*, *The Beverly Hillbillies*, *Murder She Wrote* etc. – however accurate they may or may not have been. And let's not forget the TBS's laudable movie series about famous Native Americans or the ground breaking *Northern Exposure*. But to my knowledge, no particular show or series dealing specifically with Aboriginal life has ever been created south of the border.

In fact, proportionally speaking, I often felt the representation of First Nations people in Canada was almost directly proportional to the portrayal of African-Americans in the States. In America, since the 1960's, there were and are lots of television shows about the "Black" experience, again, however accurate. But no Native people. Now try and find an ongoing series about the Black community on Canadian television – *Air Farce*, *This Hour Has 22 Minutes*, *Black Harbour*, *Traders* etc., all exploring the mysterious and unknown world of Caucasian Canada. Do you realize there are more television shows on the air right now about aliens from outer space than about Native people? They must have a better agent than we do.

But attempting to be optimistic, perhaps this was just a dip in the cultural graph of television reality. George Anthony, one of the major shareholders in the CBC Brain trust, also informed me that CBC Children's is planning "two new series – *Inuk* and *Stories from the Seventh Fire*. *Inuk*, based on the work of acclaimed artist and illustrator Marc Tetro, is a show about an imaginative eight year old Inuit boy who is destined to be a Shaman. Stories From *The Seventh Fire* is a half hour animated (2D and 3D) and live action retelling of Native stories."

And rumours of a new *North Of Sixty* movie and some new series called "*Harry's Case*" with Adam Beach as a side kick may prove me wrong in the end. Perhaps there's hope after all. The spirit of *The Beachcomber's* Jesse Jim may ride again.

Keeping all this in mind, it's easy to understand how the introduction of the Aboriginal Peoples Television Network has changed the playing field substantially. Where else can you go to see re-runs of *Adventures in Rainbow Country* and that classic of Canadian identity, *The Forest Rangers*? As innovative and ground-breaking as APTN's creation was, in its zeal to find suitable (i.e. Native tinted) and inexpensive programming, the fledgling network's options were a tad limited.

When it originally went on the air several years ago, most of the programming came from the voluminous archives of the North, where the Inuit Broadcasting Corporation and northern CBC affiliates in Iqaluit, Yellowknife and Whitehorse had been storing away programs about the changing face of the Aboriginal north for decades. My mother swore after watching the first few months of the network that she never wanted to see another Inuit/Dene hunting or seal/caribou gutting again.

Debra Piapot, APTN'S Director of Communications, proudly hails the birth of the new network as being "an acknowledgement of the Grandmothers and Grandfathers of television broadcasting if you will, who brought forth and had this dream of including all of Canada's Aboriginal people to start this network." Their dream for the future – "We want to be world class and relevant. Ratings aside, if we're not relevant to each other, then we've already lost the battle, but if we do talk to each other and we are engaged in entertaining, and are relevant and authentic to each other, I think the ratings will go up. The rest of Canada will begin to watch."

To it's credit, the network has become increasingly confident and experienced, and more interesting and broad based shows have been making their appearance. It's two current affairs programs, *Invision* and *Contact*, carry all the news a First Nations person should know. The talk show *Buffalo Tracks* and the self-explanatory *Cooking with The Wolfman* all add variety to the programming. However, broadcasting *Shining Time Station* and *Dudley the Dragon*, only because they star Tom Jackson and Graham Greene, might need to be re-evaluated. And if I see either *Thunderheart* or *Billy Jack* aired one more time...

James Compton, the Director of Programming for the APTN network, has had his own less-than-stellar experiences searching for corporate answers to why there are less tanned faces on a publicly funded network like the CBC, one that is suppose to represent the country's multi–faceted population. "I was at the Banff Television Executive Program, there you have representatives from Vision, History, CTV, CBC, BBC, the cream of the crop, all sharing ideas on how to run a Network."

"CBC came in with their fall launch, what they were planning to do in the upcoming year. When they showed us the promotional tape, I decided to count how many times they showed Native people. It was only a five minute video and I counted twenty-six shots of Aboriginal people. I said "does this mean you're planning to do more Native programming?" Well, that went over like a fart in Church. It was like I stabbed them in the heart. They didn't really answer the question, basically skirted the issue. Most of the shots were from the history series anyways."

But things are beginning to change, at least south of the border. And it all started with that call I received in the wilds of Lethbridge. American television may be waking up while Canadian television is going to sleep. That was the National Broadcasting Corporation, as in NBC – as in the NBC – that had called me.

It seems the network had recently polled its audiences and were shocked (their words – "shocked") to discover they had no programming for or about American Indians! And they wanted to do something about it. I was shocked that they were shocked. It seemed rather obvious to me – no more a revelation than 'lard is fattening.'

This American gentleman from New York who had found me in the Alberta prairies was on a quest to find Native people in the industry who might be interested in submitting material to the Network and work with them on dealing with this "shocking" imbalance. Thus the phone call.

We had a twenty minute conversation in the airport about

the issue and all its potential ramifications until they started boarding my plane. And for a moment, I seriously debated missing my flight to continue this interesting conversation... after all, it was NBC, and they had phoned me. Me! NBC or Saskatoon... now there's a choice you don't make very often.

That was two months ago. Now NBC is taking a more broad based approach to deal with this disproportional situation. The Network, along with the Onieda Indian Nation in Wisconsin, is launching a talent search for Native American actors, comedians and writers. Called "The Four Directions Talent Search," it aims to increase Native representation in television, and will take place across the United States and Canada, between August and November 2001.

The press release has been all over the internet in Indian country the last few days and the buzz has started. People on the Reserves can taste the Emmys. While the Prime Minister and Parliament has been worried about the brain drain of scientists and skilled technicians to the south, who would have thought there might be a similar exodus of Native artists and performers in the not too distant future.

Granted, right now it's a glorified talent search, an ethnic cattle call of humongous proportion. But its something, a beginning. Just think, our own series snuggled between *Ally McBeal* and *Friends*. Between *Fraser* and *Law & Order*. I think the show should either be called *Touched By An Anglo* or *Cree's Company*.

ANNA MAE
The Woman, The Legend, The Media

"The whole country changed with only a handful of raggedy-ass pilgrims that came over here in the 1500's. And it can take a handful of raggedy-ass Indians to do the same and I intend to be one of those raggedy-ass Indians." Anna Mae Aquash

"Do you want to be a martyr?" *Anna Mae's Movement*

Not a lot of Native women from a small Micmac Reserve in Nova Scotia end up murdered and buried on the wind-swept plains of South Dakota. Even fewer become international icons. The saga of Anna Mae Aquash nee' Pictou, in the thirty years she lived and the twenty six years since she died, continues to enamor and captivate the public.

She has become a symbol of tragedy and bravery that will undoubtedly outlive all those who knew her. In the years since her body was found in a ditch, a bullet in the back of her head, she has become larger in death than she probably would have been in life – despite her political commitment and much venerated compassion. Martyrdom is often more sexy than any of the above. Ask Joan of Arc.

South Dakota, early and mid 1970's. A civil war is in progress on the Pine Ridge Reservation between corrupt Band officials assisting the FBI, and traditionalist Indians, supported by the American Indian Movement (AIM). Aquash is caught in the middle of the anarchy. Tensions run high. People are accusing other people of being spies for the FBI. There are deaths almost weekly. Including, finally, Anna Mae's in December 1975.

Her murderer? Still officially a mystery, though new revelations point to AIM members driven to paranoia by FBI whisper campaigns - again like Joan of Arc, who was betrayed by her own people. Her story practically drips with dramatic potential.

A few weeks ago in Toronto, Canada's premiere Aboriginal theatre company, Native Earth Performing Arts Inc., remounted a play about the fabled Anna Mae, written and directed by the talented Yvette Nolan. *Annie Mae's Movement* is an attempt to tell her detailed story in ninety minutes. The performances of the two leads were wonderful, the set imaginative, but alas Nolan's clever direction was stronger than the text.

The major problem with the play came from the larger-than-life scenario it draws from. Anybody familiar with her story or who had thumbed through Peter Mattheissen's *In The Spirit Of Crazy Horse*, knows everything that was going to befall her. That's the trouble with writing about a legend – we learn what we already know, but it leaves us wondering what we don't know.

In other dramatized stories based on historical events, like *Saving Private Ryan* which takes place during World War II's Normandy invasion, viewers clearly had at least a glimmer of how the war would later turn out and who eventually won. The secret was to place a smaller, more intimate story within the larger scope of destruction. A microcosm inside a macrocosm. Unfortunately *Anna Mae's Movement* felt more like a good documentary. Or more interestingly, a canonization. A contemporary Joan of Arc.

Often with figures the community holds dear, writers are afraid to fudge the details or to play with the truth. One of the first things a dramatic writer is told is that reality is a great inspiration but it doesn't make for a finished script.

Several years ago, I was hired by a film company to write a made-for-TV movie about a Native man from Manitoulin Island who went hunting and got lost in the woods for ten days. The OPP suspended search efforts after three days but the people of his community kept looking until the tenth day, when they felt there was no hope. As they were packing up on that final day, the lost man walked out of the woods. A true story, full of dramatic potential.

I wrote the first draft, sticking to the facts and details. Then I met with the producer. He said it was a good start but was very emphatic in pointing out that he wasn't paying me to write a documentary. He told me to find the human element, the small-er, more intimate story that personified the man, not tell the tale of a lost hunter surviving against nature. History lessons bored him, he said.

But Anna Mae's Movement is just the latest in a series of projects, eager to explore those explosive 70's events. Most famous was the Michael Apted movie, *Thunderheart*, staring Val Kilmer and Graham Greene. Here, the character based on Anna Mae Pictou Aquash, played by Sheila Tousey, wound up face down in a shallow grave, AIM founder and poet John Trudell, who figured largely in Aquash's life, also starred in the film.

But while the film was set in South Dakota in the middle of the same low-intensity conflicts that killed Aquash, the script plays fast and loose with the facts. The main character is a mixed blood Lakota FBI agent who discovers his roots, demonstrating that there are an infinite number of ways to spin the AIM epic. Aquash's life and the circumstances of her death have now become fodder for the artists to examine and shape. Myth mak-ers, get your laptops ready.

APTN - HAPPY BIRTHDAY

What do a legal will kit (for when you're dead), a watch with a cat emblem on its face, a songs-from-the-60's CD collection, a magic wallet, and a device that allows you to hang 200% more shirts and other clothing in your limited closet space, have in common? These are all television ads recently broadcast on the new Aboriginal Peoples Television network. It makes me wonder if all the big ad agencies in Canada think Native people as a whole are all overdressed, feline-obsessed, wealthy ex-hippies waiting to die. Evidently I'm not alone.

With APTN barely into its second year of existence, I guess the people working in the APTN Sales and Marketing department can't afford to be too picky when it comes to selling air time. When the network started up, there was little money to be had for much original programming, and an all Aboriginal network would be new territory for ad agencies to explore and study. But basically, I have some difficulty envisioning GAP sponsoring *Kiviu's Journey*, or seeing a Mercedes Benz commercial during *Kippinguijautiit*, and I won't even touch the implications of Labatt's or Molson's buying advertising space in the middle of *Medicine Wheel*.

That's just one of the multitude of problems that running a brand new Aboriginal network can entail. Programming being number one on the list. After surfing to Channel 72 (in Toronto) during the past year, I discovered that between those interesting commercials, you can while away hour after hour after hour viewing an endless parade of documentaries or current affairs shows. Everything, and I do mean everything you needed to know about Aboriginal life, from trapping in the Yukon, right down to what the Micmacs are wearing this spring, can be found on the Native network.

Dramatically, there still needs to be some serious theatrical development instituted. But as all television executives know, drama is a hell of a lot more expensive, several times over in fact, than a news show. As it stands now, APTN airs a fifteen year old television series called *Spirit Bay*, or occasionally a twenty year old pseudo-Indian movie.

Every Saturday and Sunday, you can watch a mainstream children's series called *Shining Time Station* where one of the stars happens to be Native but the trains never arrive on time because of 'Indian time.' Gripping Native programming? Not exactly cutting edge stuff to make CTV or CBC long for the days when the only Natives on television were Italians and Spanish.

I say fight fire with fire. I want to see some dynamic programming that rocks the proverbial canoe. Native people are just as familiar with sex and violence as white people and the main networks. Perhaps even more so. You should have been at my 35th birthday party.

I say to the new network "let's show them how to do it Aboriginal style." We need shows like *Pride and Passion In Pikangikum* or *Sex and Success in Sucker Creek*. I personally would put money into *Hudson's Baywatch*.

Maybe then, I wouldn't have to keep scrambling for a pen to write down the number for that Kitty Kat watch. And perhaps more importantly, why is it that "this item is not available in stores?"

ELECTRONIC SMOKE SIGNALS

It has been said that the three most amazing things ever invented by the white culture are the air conditioner, the push up bra
and television. However, many of those same people (and quite
a few others) would argue that television has done almost as
much, if not more, to damage Native culture than Residential
schools and country music combined.

It's no secret that in many First Nation communities, pop
culture has replaced Native culture to a terrifying degree. The
television has become omnipotent. Take a personal poll of your
friends and ask how many of them know by heart the words to
Gilligan's Island or *The Brady Bunch*? And then, ask how many
of them know a traditional Ojibway/Cree/Iroquois/etc. song? Or
even a traditional story. Proportionally, I'd think you'd have a
better chance of winning bingo.

As further proof, all across this country that used to be ours
(including the U.S.), you cannot go to a village or town, however isolated, where a hefty percentage of both the children and
adults do not wear wrestling T-shirts, or other clothing inspired
by the pervasiveness of the broadcast media. But try and find a
Cooking with The Wolfman sweat pants and you'll get my meaning. Caucasian broadcasting has ruled our communities for
almost fifty years. I remember growing up on the Reserve
watching television at my grandparents. My first impression of
the "outside world" consisted of watching *Captain Kangaroo*
and The Three Stooges. Those were early role–models till my
mother warned me about older men with their "tickle trunks".

As a result, television has also been accused of lending a
helping hand in destroying the already fragile hold Aboriginal
languages still have in our communities. Generations of little

children watching Oscar the Grouch, Bert and Ernie speak all that English with a little French occasionally thrown in, when traditionally, they should have been out on the land, hunting down the relatives of Big Bird. One bird the size of him could keep a community like Saugeen fed for a week.

But I don't believe this dominance of the airwaves has to continue this way. Like anything, television can have both a negative and positive influence. As the wise old Japanese Elder from *The Karate Kid* says (which I confess I did see recently on television), "no such thing as a bad student, only a bad teacher." Television is what you make it. With the Aboriginal Peoples Television Network now telling our stories our way, could there possibly be an Indigenous light at the end of the cultural tunnel?

With organizations like The Centre for Aboriginal Media calling the shots these days, not to mention the success of the Aboriginal Peoples Television Network, the winds are definitely shifting. It's been almost a year since APTN signed on the air and we're all sitting in front of the television waiting in eager anticipation of the ground-breaking film, video and television to tell our stories our way.

Instead of *Gilligan's Island*, it could be *Wapole Island*, *Lennox Island*, *Georgina Island*, *Christian Island*, or all of *Manitoulin Island* or that matter. Casting the large Skipper wouldn't be that difficult. And is it only me or can you hear this television theme song on APTN: "Here's the story, of a man named Beardy..."

EVIDENTLY I'VE BEEN A BAD, BAD BOY

It's beginning to look like the year 2000 is going to be a very interesting year for yours truly, the humble Ojibway scribe. As a writer in many disciplines, I primarily write for theatre, television and journalism. Now seemingly, I have been a very naughty boy in all three branches of literary expression; a few people finding fault with each genre of my examination of the Aboriginal world. And all I can do is sit there and just shake my head in disbelief. In my simple attempts to just make people laugh, I have inadvertently created some wrinkled brows and scowling faces.

It's only April, and in the last four months, I've received a bomb threat for a play of mine in Vancouver that an anonymous caller said was racist against white people, followed by a children's television show I have been writing for telling me quite explicitly that I am not to use the teachings of tobacco in any script I may write for them. And finally, an article I wrote for the Messenger, the AFN paper, has been banned and dropped for the spring issue. Evidently I am an irritant and didn't even know it. Could my ex-girlfriend be right?

The bomb threat, luckily a false one, said my play, *alterNATIVES*, made fun of white people. Odd, considering I am half white, half of the cast was white, and the Native characters in it had their own set of problems. All the characters were screwed up, in my opinion, much like real life. But the play was funny. But social criticism and humour evidently are not suppose to go together. I'm thirty seven and still have so much to learn. And worst of all, my mother found out about the bomb threat and gave me a good scolding, telling me to "start writing good plays again!" Yes, mother.

The children's show I was writing for (I cannot name them since I was told there were confidentiality issues at stake here and legal recourse was possible – people are so serious these days!) wouldn't allow me to mention, in one simple line that would involve no more than a second and a half of screen time, anything about tobacco. One of the characters wanted something (nothing greedy, more of a personal wish) and I wanted an Elder-type character to suggest the young character put down some tobacco as an offering, in keeping with the teachings.

Children's show. Tobacco. The two do not go well in the minds of the television networks. Even though I was talking about Indian tobacco, leaf with no chemicals, not cigarette tobacco. Again we're talking one simple line of dialogue. Apparently it was an irrelevant issue. No different I guess than the wine you find in a bar and the wine you find at Communion. Again I have so much still to learn.

And finally, I wrote an article for the Messenger examining mixed marriages, primarily focusing on non-Native people who, because of their new current marital affiliation, now refer to themselves as being "Native." It was a situation I once heard referred to as "Indian by Ejaculation." Again, it was done with humour and what I hoped was keen social observation. But it was just more evidence that I was being a bad boy. Must have been all those George Carlin records I listened to as a kid.

I was asked to cut out several sections that they felt might offend some family members, particularly the "ejaculation" reference. That was a surprise to me because I was under the impression, however wrongly, that "ejaculation" was a real and legitimate word. I've even looked it up in the dictionary and everything. It's there, I assure you. I'm also quite sure I've actually read the word in a few academic articles and in some literary prose (not that I read a lot of writing that has the word "ejaculation" in it. Honest!).

Also a reference to a Jewish circumcision met with some unexpected resistance. Is it me or am I noticing a theme in that office's uncomfortability?

Be that as it may, I was willing to change the "ejaculation" to "intercourse" to be supportive but I was told it wasn't enough. I was told the article was being dumped. I hope my mother doesn't find out about this one. She's been hinting about lawn furniture for Mother's day and I may not be able to afford it if these unfortunate events keep up.

Taking all this into consideration, these incidents boggle my mind, and I assure you, it takes a lot to boggle my mind. As far as writers go, I've always considered myself a rather innocuous writer, as agitators go. I have not advocated the blowing up of one single bridge in my entire career, or have I ever supported any Native terrorist organizations. Nor did I expect to ever consider myself becoming the Ojibway version of Salman Rushdie.

So being the bad, evil, naughty writer I am, have I learned anything from this experience? Are there any words of wisdom I can pass on to others should they find themselves in a similar situation? Yeah. Asked to be paid up front.

Mental Note – Start all future articles/plays/scripts with a warning: The following is meant to be funny. Do not take it seriously.

THE POLITICS OF CHILDREN

I'm a thirty-seven year old man, single child of a single parent, who at the time of this writing has no children (though the summer of '87 seems kind of foggy), and what's the one job that comes to mind that I would be completely unsuited for. Other than an aerobics instructor (though I do look good in spandex, if the lighting is low enough)?

I am talking about my recent splurge of writing specifically for children in television and on the stage. And let me tell you Mr. Mathew Coon Comb, running the Assembly of First Nations with over 600 squabbling and arguing Chiefs and Vice-Chiefs is nothing compared to the trials and tribulations of pleasing networks and producers in the fast paced and bizarre world of entertaining and educating the little ones.

In the past, I have had some experience. I've written at least four plays for young audiences (maybe more, as I said, the summer of '87 is still a little foggy). My first was a rather surprising hit called *Toronto At Dreamer's Rock* which, ten years later, is still being produced and published. I affectionately refer to it as my retirement fund.

But more recently, I have been engaged in the lucrative, though frustrating world of children's television programming. Specifically, I have written three scripts for a Native-themed show involving animals, currently in production. I had a lot of fun and everybody was really nice to me... until the rules came down from somewhere above about what you can and can not do on Children's television. Sort of the Television Ten Commandments. And some of them are bizarre. As a writer, I was only privileged to snippets of reasoning. Basically, anything beyond "don't do that" or "nice try but you can't do that with a turtle at 11:00 o'clock in the morning" was kept confidential. Evidently the television executive's mind works in mysterious ways.

Abbreviating the Commandments, I was frequently told that you cannot have any violence, even a kick in the shin or a push. Now that kind of stuff you can almost understand. But did you know, you cannot have one character kiss another on the nose as I attempted to write in one script? It might corrupt the Aboriginal (and non-Aboriginal youth) of tomorrow. There might be rampant nose kissing across the nation. The courts would be clogged with nasal assault cases.

Other no-no's imparted to me included the fact that you cannot have one character call another character "weird" in an effort to explore self-image problems. Not even if you show the potential consequences of such an action. It seems it's better to avoid the whole situation completely. Yet, its okay to have a male animal tug on the tail of a female animal. Am I the only one that sees some subversive subtext in a little "pulling tail?"

Luckily in theatre, its a little easier. Actually a lot easier. I can safely say that, other than the normal dramaturgical process of developing the play, I never really received any flack or limiting directives from a higher up source. I even began my favourite play, *Girl Who Loved Her Horses*, with one of the main characters uttering a single word in astonishment: "Jesus!" Try that with the Teletubbies at 8:30 on Tuesday morning.

Granted, you still have to keep your audience in mind and what you are trying to say. Artistic freedom is artistic freedom, but spending fifty minutes of school time having characters swearing like a Chief who's been caught hiring relatives or wasting time exploring the wonders of bestiality would not be advisable. That's just common sense.

More recently, I have been working on a new young people's play titled *The Boy In The Treehouse* which will be seen in Winnipeg, Toronto, Saskatoon and Regina. It deals with identity, parental longing, trying to honour ones relatives and vision quests. I was tempted to put in some tail-pulling but somehow it did not seem appropriate.

I had not written a children's play in about five years and wasn't sure if I could capture that state of mind again. Writing for children is a unique and special talent. But as a former girlfriend once told me, I have nothing to worry about when it comes to thinking like a child. Oddly enough, I don't think she was the first girlfriend to tell me that.

In this play, a young boy must deal with the anniversary of the death of his Native mother by trying to embrace her culture. He does this by fasting in a treehouse. His non-Native father tries to be supportive but watching your kid starve himself up a tree tests the man's patience. In this piece, I got to explore concepts that many youth deal with. And as always, I was told the sky was the limit. Just the usual limitations when it comes to a touring show: not too many characters and try not to require a full scale castle or naval battle – they're kind of hard to tour. The only real concern I faced with this project was a kind and gentle word of advice from the Artistic Director informing me that people in certain parts of the Prairies are kind of serious about any mention of God or the Church.

But perhaps the most bizarre limitation that I was informed of did not come from any network executive or Artistic Director, but from the people who run kindergardens. My former girlfriend taught kindergarten for four months a few years back. It was a job she loved, almost as much as she loved the kids. But she was warned, and strongly urged never to hug the kids. Even if they hugged her first, at no time was her arms or hands to touch the kids in an affectionate manner. She told me it was the hardest part of her job.

Then a few months later when I was in Labrador, I had the opportunity to tour the schools in a Native community, including a kindergarten. Over coffee, I chatted with the teachers about my girlfriends delimna. They informed me they had the same regulations. "But we ignore them" they happily told me. Unfortunately I was all too aware of the reasoning behind these restrictions, and sympathetic. But another part of me wished my girlfriend could hug all these kids as much as she wanted to.

So remember, anybody out there who is interested in writing or working with kids; under no circumstances should you hug a nose-kissing, weird, Church-going kid. No telling what trouble you'll get into.

DESPERATELY SEEKING SOLUTIONS

Over the past several years I have written many articles discussing the concept of the "blended blood" issue in the Native community. In fact, I have even been admonished by one Elder to, and I quote, "get over it." Evidently I am dangerously close to becoming the poster boy for People of Mixed Societies (otherwise known as PMS). If the truth be told, I have actually gotten over whatever "it" is, many years ago and revel in my unique perspective of the world. It's cheaper than therapy. However, every once in a while the whole damn issue raises its head yet again wanting another opportunity to be hotly debated.

No doubt we've all drank far too much tea participating in these discussions about what makes an Indian an Indian. Is it nature or nurture? Is it time spent on a Reserve, or a simple matter of blood quantum as is popular in the States? Maybe its the inherent ability to fascinate anthropologists. Or perhaps some indefinable combination of the three?

But this time I've decided to hang up my blanket on the issue and let other people answer this question for me. I've done enough talking (or in this case, writing) to last a life time. I've decided to look for answers out there in the grass roots communities.

The reason for this departure? A certain someone has approached me with difficult questions relating to this particular concern. And since my mother has frequently told me I am not all powerful or all knowing, I've decided to openly seek assistance.

Last year, Lee Maracle, Dawn T. Maracle (no relation) and I were having coffee one day when the topic of Native literature genres was brought up. We observed that Native writers seemed preoccupied with writing only about certain things, usually contemporary stories, on contemporary Reserves leading contemporary lives. Occasionally there might be a legend, or a historical/period piece, or something tackling the mystical/mythological/philosophical side of Aboriginal life (i.e. If an Indian farts in the bush and a white person isn't there to hear him, has he actually farted?)

A vast part of our literature deals primarily with looking backward, to our ancestors, at our culture, our language, our history, the colonization, the struggle to recover, etc. Usually, it explores or recounts the past and its relation to the present. Very little speculative work in the other direction has been created. We ended up discussing the topic of First Nations science fiction. There is precious little out there today. Gerry William's *The Black Ship* and the odd short story here and there are about all we came across in Canada.

Examples outside of Canada, even flying high above it where no Native has gone before, is Chakotey, the guy on Star Trek's Voyager. Basically I always thought of him as a Latino with a bad tattoo. They don't even mention what Nation he's from or how a self respecting First Nations person could honour the Four Directions while deep in space. Which way is East? Towards the phaser banks I think.

Getting back to the point, Dawn T. Maracle decided to tackle this unusual literary possibility and is currently looking for Native authors interested in writing a Science Fiction short story for a planned anthology. It is hoped this book, for a change, will look forward to the future of the Aboriginal Nation. While searching for interested participants, she has landed smack dab in the middle of a dilemma – one dealing with that pesky identity issue.

A woman has offered to write a story for the anthology, but she has readily admitted that a distant ancestor (one of these all too familiar forbearers who's first name often started with "Great-great-") was the proud owner of some Aboriginal blood, but she herself had never lived on a Reserve and hadn't delved that deeply into her "great-great" culture. So the question facing Dawn T. Maracle is – Should she allow this woman to write a story for the Anthology? And expanding on that particular issue, what are the guidelines for making a decision like this?

God forbid we do not want to go back to the ill defined and nasty Department of Indian Affairs classifications; Status, non-Status or Métis. But at the same time, there must be some quality and accuracy control to make sure it is in fact the Native voice born of the Native experience writing these stories. It would be tacky to start out the new Millennium with an updated W.P. Kinsella or Grey Owl.

Gerald Taiaiake Alfred, a Mohawk academic, uses the colourful metaphor of a Canadian flying to Germany, getting off the plane and self identifying himself/herself as a German, thinking that's sufficient. Needless to say that wouldn't be nearly enough for the Germans. I've been to Germany. They require just a tiny bit more documentation. And it works in reverse. Some stranger showing up at an airport Customs office wanting to enter Canada simply by saying "I'm Canadian" just doesn't cut the mustard anymore. So why should that be good enough for the Native community, he asks. Simply saying "I am Native" isn't enough anymore.

On the other hand, the Aborigines of Australia have their own unique methods of determining who is what, and vice versa. Basically, as I have been told, you are considered Aborigine if 1) you have some Aborigine ancestry, 2) you self-identify yourself as being Aborigine, and 3) the Aborigine community acknowledges you as being Aborigine. It sounds logical but cynics have pointed out that anybody and their grandmother (or Great-Great-Grandmother) could consider themselves Aborigine. And Ted, the Aborigine down the street who runs the local gas station could say that for $20, he (as a member of the community) will recognize you as being Aborigine.

Therefore, I ask the readers out there – what do you suggest we take into account? I dare you to pick up a pen/keyboard/telephone to provide us poor confused people some guidance and intelligent suggestions to help us define this thorny problem. Contact us and inform us of what you think the essentials of the Aboriginal voice are.

We humbly await your response.

ADVENTURES IN THE SKIN TRADE

One of the most influential books I ever read was called *Adventures In The Screen Trade* by William Goldman, the guy who wrote the movies *Misery* and *Butch Cassidy and the Sundance Kid*. In it, he recounts the wonderful, magical, annoying, horrifying and eventually unique adventures professional scriptwriters have plying their trade in Hollywood. Many of us who toil away as contemporary storytellers here in Canada were relieved to know it wasn't just us who felt like we were carving marble masterpieces using only a chisel and our foreheads as hammers.

As a First Nations writer, the battles become a distinctive story on their own. In my career I have survived such literary questions as "Do Native People really do that?" in reference to a section I once wrote where a Native interpretation of *Star Trek* ethics is discussed at a dinner party. "Wouldn't they normally be talking about something more important like Self Government or something?"

I did a quick and dirty poll of several Aboriginal friends and came up with the startling conclusion that of the twelve or so people I questioned (from as wide and varied background as I could arrange), four fifths could remember talking about *Star Trek* in some form or matter in the recent past, while only one had mentioned Self Government in a social environment, only because she had been asked a question by a non-Native dinner guest. It makes me wonder if white people only discuss white issues like whether Reform Party members wear boxers or briefs.

Last summer I had the unique pleasure of watching a half hour drama I wrote for television be produced. It was called *The*

Strange Case Of Bunny Weequod, and it was sort of an Aboriginal X Files, involving a Native man being kidnapped by the Little People and then being sent out on a mission. But during pre-production, we decided to do something different with this particular project, to set it aside from all other productions. To the best of our knowledge, this production was the first film, to be broadcast on CBC, written, directed, produced, and staring Native people, and completely in an Aboriginal language – Ojibway to be exact. The only words of English left in the script were "Hank Williams Jr." – evidently there is no suitable translation.

In the process we all learned something new, or more exactly, something we already knew but never had a practical example of. For instance, the normal length of a half hour drama for television is approximately twenty-five to thirty pages for twenty-two or twenty-three minutes of air time (the additional pages allows elbow room for editing). Because the structure of the words and sentences is radically different in Ojibway than English, the final length of the Ojibway script ended up being 42 pages of Aboriginal eloquence. It seems us Ojibways are much longer winded than I had realized.

Now estimate a shooting script coming down to approximately one page for every minute on the screen. You begin to see the problem. Forty-two pages for twenty-two minutes resulted in serious editing of the script with the final product being screened with only the bare bones of the story surviving. Add to that three of the four actors not being Ojibway, and you get an idea of some of the fun we had during the production. Pretty soon the whole cast began to see little people.

All problems aside, we all eagerly awaited the broadcast of our special little production, now outfitted with English subtitles. We waited and waited. I believe it was on a Wednesday that the CBC finally called us, four months later, informing us it was going to be aired in four days. On a Sunday. At 11:30 at night. Part of a little known series called *Canadian Reflections*. All this meant that with only four days warning, no advance publicity to alert and inform the television watching public was done.

As a result, only about forty-two people all across Canada saw *The Strange Case of Bunny Weequod*, of which only about three could probably understand it (all relatives). Contractually, the CBC is required to air it three more times by next fall. Hopefully with more than four days notice or I'm putting a land claim on the CBC (like anybody will notice).

Luckily the last project I've been working on has been a little more compliant. I was asked to write a Public Service Announcement (called a PSA) on anti-Racism for the Centre of Aboriginal Media. My concept was of an old cowboy and western movie, five noble warriors riding up in horses. The Chief talks very stereotypically about attacking a wagon train and taking scalps. But the other warriors rebel against the stereotype by commenting that traditionally, they didn't take scalps, or the fact they are riding in zero degree weather with only a thin buckskin vest on.

It was a hoot to work on, even as reality itself made an appearance to prove the point of the PSA. None of the five Native actors hired to do the scene had ever ridden a horse before. Except for one actor, who I'm told was the first to be bucked. Another stereotype of the proud Indian bites the dust - literally.

It was a thirty second PSA so for obvious reasons, I didn't use any Ojibway.

WHITE LIKE ME

This week I learned something I had hitherto been unaware of. According to a theatre review in Vancouver's *Georgia Strait* by Colin Thomas and one irate social commentator who has the ability to make a phone call, I was potentially a "racist," as evidenced by the review title: "Witless white-bashing". This headline, and the text that followed, indicate that I used my play, *alterNATIVES*, as a pedestal from which to lambaste and criticize members of the Caucasian race. Further evidence that I really must learn to reread my plays before having them produced. I sometimes miss the strangest things.

And to top this whole bizarre issue off, it has been indicated that my play, and the critical review that followed, may or may not have been responsible for a bomb threat that cancelled one evening's show at the Firehall Arts Centre. The theatre received a anonymous phone call warning if the theatre is "going to do racist plays, [they] shouldn't be surprised if [they] found something in the theatre." So much for Vancouver being more laid back than Toronto.

I have read Mr. Thomas' review and in several places, he does seem unusually harsh about his interpretations of the six characters (three Native, three non–Native). One of my purposes in writing this play is that I was once criticized for always writing "nice" characters, or more specifically that I had never created unsympathetic characters. That was one of the functions of my play – to create three dimensional people with opposing viewpoints that might shake things up a bit. Evidently I was a little too effective.

This issue also brings to mind the age-old expression that wisely suggests "Never blame a writer for what his characters may say." Personally I think that's true but then again, maybe I just have an axiom to grind.

While, indeed, the white characters are the butt of many jokes in my play, the Native characters are no less sympathetic. Trust me. In fact, because they are more often than naught the instigators of the comedic persecution, they come off more dislikable than the non-Native characters. During an early workshop of the play, a Native female acquaintance came up to me, somewhat indignantly, and angrily asked me if that was my attitude towards all Native people, referring to the unsympathetic portrayal. She felt it was too one-sided in favour of the white characters. It seems I'm damned if I do, and damned if I don't.

And as for me personally having something against white people (and believe it or not, some of my best friends are white – I've had lunch with them and everything), obviously Mr. Thomas hasn't laid eyes on me. For if we were to meet on the street, I can practically guarantee he would undoubtably mistake me for a member of that race of people known as Occidental/Caucasian/white. My blue eyes would attest to my membership, so it makes little sense that I would waste two hours of precious stage time making fun of twelve of my twenty-four chromosomes. I'm not that much in need of therapy.

I can, however, understand what appears to be a growing sense of intolerance out on the West Coast. We here in the East continue to hear about the feelings of indignation towards First Nations people. Witness the anger and confusion surrounding the Nisga'a Treaty business, not to mention the Musqueam leaseholder issue. I know for a fact Montreal and Quebec went through the same disorientation after Oka. And of course, Aboriginal arts is one of the most public displays of culture available, as well as the most vulnerable.

While this is my first bomb threat (but hopefully my final), it will probably not be my last bad review. That is the nature of the business. And in all fairness to Colin Thomas, he has been more than generous in his reviews of my past work. Of course that was back in my pre-racist days. I think I will spend the rest of the day trying to come up with the Native equivalent of a skinhead (how about a buck-skinhead?).

Well, at least my mother will be happy. She always wanted me to make something of myself.

Drew HaydenTaylor is an Ojibway/Caucasian (better known as an Occasion) playwright who is looking forward to seeing his play tonight. He will be the one wearing the red sheet.

LAUGHING TILL YOUR FACE IS RED

"A smile is Sacred"
Hopi Elder

It seems some people have no sense of humour. I am tempted to say some "white people" but that would be racist. Though I'm told that it is politically impossible for a member of an oppressed minority to be racist against a dominant culture because of some socio-political reason... but I digress.

A year or two ago, a play of mine titled *alerNATIVES* was produced in Vancouver. I don't know why I was so surprised by the Non-Native reaction to Native humour, specifically that presented in theatre, has always been something of a perception problem, as the art form continues to grow. With the ongoing debate over the suitability of political correctness, the dominant culture's willingness to enjoy, appreciate and accept the unique Native sense of humour quickly becomes a political mine field. Add to that the volatile atmosphere existing in British Columbia at that time by the fall out over the Nisga'a Treaty and the turmoil involving the Musqueam landowners, and it's no wonder a few people in Vancouver were less than enthused by a Native comedy/drama and began developing theatre appraisal via chemical interaction.

But looking at the larger picture, this particular reaction to Native humour goes beyond Vancouver and last December, at least in my experience. Several years ago I was fortunate enough to have an early play of mine produced at the Lighthouse Theatre in Port Dover, Ontario. It was a small, innocuous comedy called *The Bootlegger Blues* which detailed the adventures of a fifty-eight year old, good Christian Ojibway woman named

Martha, who through a series of circumstances, finds herself bootlegging 143 cases of beer to raise money to buy an organ for the Church. Not exactly Sam Sheppard but it was based on an actual real incident that happened on a Reserve that for legal reasons I won't get into or my mother will kill me.

In this play there were no searing insights in the Aboriginal existence, or tragic portrayals of a culture done-wrong-by that we have grown to expect on the stage. In fact, it was the opposite of that. The director/dramaturge with whom I developed the project, my mentor Larry Lewis, came to me one day after having just directed the premiere of this little play you may have heard of, *Drylips Oughta Move to Kapiskasing*. He was somewhat burnt out by the process and said to me "Drew, I want you to write something for me that has people leaving the theatre holding their sore stomachs from laughing so much, not drying their eyes from crying or scratching their heads from thinking too much." Thus was born *The Bootlegger Blues*.

This play, I was proud to say, had no socially redeeming qualities what so ever. It was simply, a celebration of the Native sense of humour. Not my best work in retrospect but it was funny enough to beat the theatre's audience projections and subtly (don't tell anybody) raise some awareness.

But the thing I especially remember about that particular production was that it was my first introduction to the racially divisive line that sometimes exists when a non-Native audience, is presented with Native humour, primarily on stage. Basically put, pigment-challenged audiences sometimes didn't quite know how to react to a Native comedy. And since Native theatre was still quite young, many of us Aboriginal theatre practitioners weren't too experienced in that field either. Prior to this production, The Bootlegger Blues had been produced on Manitoulin Island by a Native theatre company, so the audiences there were either primarily Native or sympathetic/interested people of pallor. After a two week run it then went on tour for a month.

In fact, it was on that tour where I received what I consider to be the best review of my life. Somewhere in Ottawa, this old man, an Elder I believe, shuffled out of seeing the play, walked up to me and shook my hand, telling me my play had made him homesick. It was then it occurred to me that maybe this play was more than just a frothy comedy.

But in Port Dover, a small town located on the shores of Lake Erie, most of the pallid theatre patrons sported white or blue-rinsed hair, and were expecting normal summer theatre epitomized by frothy British comedies or usually mindless musicals. While my humble offering was a comedy (though I hesitate to say mindless), it wasn't the type they were expecting. I still remember the discussions with the Artistic Director who was concerned about some of the "strong" language in the show. Now those that know my work can attest that I am not one of the more profane playwrights. Hell no!

The strong language consisted of, I think, one "shit" and one "F.O.A.D. (fuck off and die)" in the two hour play. But that was enough to scandalize. A wall of beer, two Indians climbing into the same bed, and a veritable plethora of jokes about alcohol and drinking from a race of people most of the audience more than likely associated with drunkenness, didn't make the situation any more accessible. And a touch uncomfortable.

But what I remember most, was the white audiences puzzled reaction to the show. It had a talented cast, and a fabulous Director. Overall, it was a very good production. You would never know by the audience response. The first ten or fifteen minutes of the play was silence. All you could hear was the cast trying vainly to engage the audience, and the audience's breathing. For all the cast's enthusiasm, this could have been a murder mystery.

I puzzled over the audience's unexpected lack of involvement for some time. I knew it couldn't be the actors or the production. Heaven forbid, was it my writing? But the show had done well on Manitoulin Island. Then after one afternoon matinee, it occurred to me. It wasn't me. It was them, the audience. Proving my point, I overheard one pigment challenged lady coming downstairs from the balcony talking to her friend saying

"I guess it's funny, but I can't help getting over the fact that if a white man had written that, he'd be in deep trouble."

That was it. Political correctness had invaded my career. Most of the audience were afraid to laugh, or were uncomfortable with the prospect of laughing at Native people, regardless of the context. After so many years of being told the miseries and tribulations we have gone through, the concept of funny or entertaining (outside the pow wow circuit) Aboriginal people was problematic. Other plays that had been produced, like Tomson Highway's, had some humour, but were darker, or more critical, and it seems that was what the audience was expecting, and I was failing to provide it.

Perhaps in some way they wanted to feel guilty by what they saw, to be kicked in the ribs by social tragedy their ancestors had caused rather than give in to the healing powers of humour. They did not expect Native people to be funny, let alone laugh at themselves. The audience had landed on Mars.

In this post-Oka society, people were still coming to grips with the concept that Native people were no longer victimized, they could be dangerous and volatile. These are notions of a definitely non-humourous nature. Maybe the wounds of Oka were still healing.

As an afterthought I considered maybe doing a quick rewrite and throwing in a rape or murder somewhere in the text to shake the patrons up. Maybe blockading the bar or bathroom, something as a reference point for the overwhelmed audience. In fact, even though the play was about an aged female bootlegger, nowhere in the play does she or anybody actually drink a beer on stage. I didn't even give the audience that.

The other interesting fact of this production was that, as I've said, it beat the projection for audience attendance. By several important percents. So, obviously people must have liked it. I started to watch the audiences more closely in an attempt to answer this conundrum, and that's where I made my second observation. After about twenty minutes into the play, people began to laugh. Finally, the politically correct non-Natives were laughing at the Native actors doing the Native comedy. Laughing a lot I might add. Above all else, true humour must be universal.

What the audience was waiting for, seeking in fact, was permission. They were looking for permission to laugh at this strange story about oppressed people that political correctness told them not to have their funny bone tickled by. As Fate would have it, in practically every audience were several Native people enjoying the show. Luckily, Port Dover is half an hour from Six Nations, one of the largest Native communities in Canada, if not the largest population wise. And with two members of the cast coming from that community, needless to say there were always a few trickling in to see their friends/relatives appear on stage. And they needed no permission to laugh. In fact, try and stop them.

In this audience of over two hundred people (on a good night), it was always the Indians who would start the chuckling and giggling. It was laughter of recognition because seldom had this world been seen outside their own kitchen. Other than the rare movie like *Pow Wow Highway*, the humourous Indian was a rarely seen though thoroughly enjoyed animal. They were used to seeing the tragic, downtrodden and victimized Indian. According to the media, that was the only kind out there.

The laughter would start out scattered, sometimes embarrassed at being the only ones laughing but eventually, the rest of the audience got the hint that this was a comedy, and they were supposed to laugh. By the end of the performance, the whole audience were enjoying the play. A round of applause and an occasional standing ovation would follow.

I think part of the catharsis was also a sense of relief from the Caucasian patrons that everything they had seen in the media wasn't always true, the fact that Native people weren't continually depressed, suppressed and oppressed. Yes, they found out, they have a sense of humour and a joy for life. That production was a learning experience for both me, the cast and I hope, the audiences.

Several years later I wrote a sequel to *The Bootlegger Blues*, called *The Baby Blues*, part of a four parts series I'm working on called *The Blues Quartet*. It's American Premiere was at Pennsylvania Centre Stage, located at Penn State University deep in the heart of Amish country. And everybody knows what theatre animals the Amish are. Not exactly optimum territory for Native theatre but I was getting paid in American dollars.

Again, this play was a celebration of Native humour in a country that knows practically nothing of its Aboriginal inhabitants post 1880 (except for Wayne Newton). Again I witnessed that awesome silence of an audience trying to connect, trying to find some neutral ground. It didn't help that there were numerous Canadianisms in the text – references to *The Beachcombers*, Canadian Tire Money, Graham Greene (for some reason, most American people thought I was referring to the English novelist, not the Iroquois actor) to name a few. But overall, I still felt it should have been an accessible play. It had been in Toronto.

I even ended up quickly putting together a glossary of Canadian and Native words with explanations i.e. sweetgrass, drumming, Oka, fancy dancing etc. to help the audience. But still, a Native comedy was difficult for them to grasp. Oddly enough, my production was sandwiched between *Man of LaMancha* and *Forever Plaid*. Maybe if my characters were insane and wore tartan, it would have been a different story.

In this case, there were precious few American Indians around to act as guides for the confused theatre customers.

One theory I came up with, then discarded, was that Native comedies being seen in a more metropolitan environment, might be a different story. Theatre patrons in urban climates tend to be more accepting and willing to embrace styles and forms of expression that perhaps are not as well known or familiar. I've seen plays with seventeenth century people trapped in a plastic room with no dialogue, just bouncing back and forth. A Native comedy then seems almost pedestrian. Yet witness the bomb threat in Vancouver and the success in Port Dover and Kincardine (maybe mad bombers don't have cottages).

Unfortunately, there's also a double-edged sword with comedies in the city. Though there are exceptions, urban companies prefer a more serious interpretation of life. As a result, most theatres companies tend not to programme comedies as they are often viewed as being too light weight and frothy. The term I have heard is "it's more summer theatre." Thus I end up in Kincardine or Port Dover trying to explain what an inter-tribal dance is.

Native theatre as a whole has developed a fair amount of cachet in the last decade. With Ian Ross winning the Governor General's Award for his play *FareWel* (which admittedly had lots of humour), and the success of Tomson Highway and Daniel David Moses to name just a few, most major theatre companies (and many of the smaller ones) try to program a certain amount of Aboriginal theatre in their line-up. But again, their preferences lean more toward the angry, dark and often disheartening view of Native life. Thus I remember one Aboriginal woman telling me that she refused to see any more Native theatre because she found them "too depressing."

More recently, I wrote the play *alterNATIVES*, a comedy/drama this time, produced in that same Port Dover theatre in that same town. Except this time, it was more than a simple comedy. It was what I called an intellectual satire, meaning it dealt with serious and complex issues, but through humour. I've always thought the best way to reach somebody wasn't through preaching or instructing, but through humour. It seems to make the message more palatable – spoon full of sugar and all that.

This time the play premiered in two different small towns with primarily non-Native audiences. The result this time was markedly different. People, again mostly non–Native, laughed from the moment the lights came up. No waiting for permission or dealing with political guilt. In a scant six years since I had last visited Port Dover, colour-denied people had learned that it's okay to laugh at Native comedies. God (who, if my ex-girlfriend was correct, is a Mohawk woman) will not strike them down and send them to work at the Department of Indian Affairs if they laugh. It's amazing what can happen in a little over half a decade. The public looks at us now as being almost three dimensional! It's astonishing what a good laugh will get you.

I think part of the reason, if not the whole reason, is the change in perceptions through the avenues of broadcasting. Analyzing the media, witness the number of television and radio programs that have embraced the Native appetite for humour. *Dance Me Outside, The Rez* – both of which were more or less successful, the delightful movie Smoke Signals, even the CBC Radio show *Dead Dog Cafe*, written and hosted by Mr. Amusing, Tom King. Substantially more programming than was seen in 1993.

Currently I am in the stages of early development for a television series of my own, a sketch comedy show titled *SEEING RED*. I see it as a combination of *Air Farce* and America's *In Living Colour*, Native oriented humour where we make fun of the perceptions and stereotypes surrounding the First Nations culture. It could be dangerous because myself and the other two writers plan to pull the leg of white people and Native people to the point of dislocation.

The CBC seem very interested and we are proceeding down the long and winding path of development and hopefully production. I think it shows a willingness of the public now not only to embrace the Aboriginal sense of humour, but also appreciate and revel in it. So much so in fact that the powers that be at the CBC have specifically told me to concentrate on Native-based sketches only, and if possible to avoid writing any sketches not dealing specifically with Native issues. Perhaps we've gone a little too far in the other direction.

Add to that the documentary I recently directed for the National Film Board of Canada on Native humour; called *Redskins, Tricksters and Puppy Stew*, and by golly, it's almost enough to make you think Canadian society has developed somewhat in the last decade. What was once the exception, has become a widely excepted rule. There is definite hope.

In my research, I have come across a term used by some Native academics to describe humour, specifically Native humour. They refer to it as "permitted disrespect." You have the other people's permission to tease or joke about them without getting into a fight. Maybe that's what some audiences need to understand. We Native writers are part of a specific community and have to answer to that community. We are allowed a certain amount of "permitted disrespect."

But it was Tom King who also told me in a recent interview that most of the negative letters the show received come from the non-Native population, most of which say something to the effect of "If you guys (the producers/writers/actors) are white, you're not funny." Then Tom would tell them that, in fact, they are Native. These people would then respond grudgingly "Oh, that's okay then."

If I'm to understand the meaning of that sentence, it's nice to know finally that you're only funny if you're Native.

Finally, people are catching on. Except in Vancouver I guess.

"It may be the one universal thing about Native Americans from tribe to tribe, is the survival humour."

Louise Erdrich.

THE VOICE OF THE PEOPLE

One of the great adventures of being a columnist is that every once in a while, people out there who actually read the articles I write, will find the time in their busy schedules to respond with a few written words of their own. This is usually delightful since its often hard to tell if anybody has the slightest interest in what you have to say or write. Occasionally the remarks are positive but more frequently, they are from people who have issues with my writing because as the old newspaper axiom goes, "people only write letters to the editor about things that upset them."

Every columnist and professional writer is used to this, or should be. Every single person in this world has an opinion and very seldom do two match up identically. It certainly has made for some interesting correspondence over the ten years or so I have been doing this.

In that time, I have written almost a hundred and fifty articles about everything ranging from Native oriented movies, to Buffy Ste-Marie, to Matthew Coon Comb, to Residential schools, to getting old, to ex-girlfriends, to being mixed–blood, to life on my Reserve, to my cat, and trying to define the essence of Native humour, just to name a few topics.

But for me, the most remarkable and harshest responses to arise from the public have come from two noticeably vocal groups which have little to do with any of the more volatile subjects I have explored. Every year, for one reason or another, I write an article about the Native perception (and mine) of vegetarianism. Usually very tongue-in-cheek and based on experience. Why vegetarians? I don't know. Maybe because my mother forced me to eat too many vegetables as a child and I'm still dealing with the emotional scars.

But I would have to say that a good third of all the letters/ emails I have received in my professional career came from irate vegetarians, of all people, who found displeasure in my humourist approach. Not from politicians I have skewered, or Nations I have teased or injustices I have examined. But vegetarians...! Perhaps all they are saying... is give peas a chance.

The second most responsive readers of my work are people who are involved now, or in the past, with members of another race/culture. Being a half-breed myself who has dated women from several ethnic backgrounds, I often ruminate about the experience and the political implications of such a union, never saying whether it was good or bad, just exploring the adventure.

Well, simply put, a lot of people don't want it explored. They find the discussion uncomfortable. Or more accurately put, I am encouraged to give inter-racial marriages a complete thumbs up (love is colour blind) or a total thumbs down (our society and blood must be protected). There seems to be very little middle ground. And God-forbid, imagine the letters I receive when I write about someone that's involved with a vegetarian from another culture...

Other critical letters, though fewer and farther between, run the critical gambit that include intelligent, well-thought out replies that have different opinions than mine and just want the opportunity to state them. I rather enjoy this type of correspondence and respect the time and effort the writer put into their notes. Other letters often have a more different grasp of... criticism.

One Native gentleman took the time to write a letter criticizing an article I wrote lamenting the poor nutritional value of all the white flour, sugar and salt that goes into Bannock/fry bread. This fellow pointed out rather strenuously that I had not included the spiritual and cultural aspects that bannock/fry bread had in Aboriginal cultures. He finished off the letter by saying I had insulted the Elders and had no consideration for their teachings. All this over a piece of bread.

Did I mention he wrote this letter from prison? And he

believed Elders were disappointed with me for writing about the high cholesterol in fry bread. Unlike whatever he did to be writing me from jail. It's a unique world out there. One, God willing, I am hoping to understand someday.

My favourite comes from a man who took the time out of his busy day to compose a letter to the editor complaining, right off the bat, that I used to write about my girlfriend far too frequently. How much longer was I "going to continue to shove my girlfriend down" the reader's throats, he inquired? I didn't realize that occasionally singing the praises of a girlfriend violated my journalistic integrity. My answer to his problem, don't read my articles then.

I now realize this may sound like that of a wounded writer whimpering in the dark... I hope not because for most people, and especially writers, criticism should be a good thing. It should be constructive, not destructive. There must be logic and thought involved, not just emotion. The written word can be very powerful.

So with that written, all you vegetarians better quit pelting my house with rotten tomatoes or I'll get my ex-girlfriend to beat you up.

IDENTITY
(Stuff Psychiatrists Will Love)

HALF EMPTY OR HALF FULL

Not that long ago, a woman from my Reserve told my ex-girl-friend, Dawn, quite casually in conversation, that Dawn and I have had it quite easy in this world because we don't look par-ticularly Native. Somehow, having a fair complexion because of our mixed blood, made the world a far easier place to exist in and we should consider ourselves lucky to have been spared the tragedies reserved for really Native-looking Natives.

At the time, we thought it quite insightful and profoundly psychic of her to tell us how uncomplicated every single minute of our lives were up until that moment, and how horribly tragic the existence of all dark-skinned, brown eyed Aboriginal's life was in comparison. Prior to then, I had somehow been unaware of my "advantaged" status in First Nations/Caucasian relations. It must have occured that day I stayed home from school.

As the Galactic Birthing Gods would have it, I had grown up on the Curve Lake Reserve in Central Ontario, with just my mother. I lived the life of any Native person in the 1960's and seventies, complete with wood stoves, water from a hand pump, all the usual accoutrement that comes with that privileged Reserve life. But at the time, nobody had ever commented on my bluish-green eyes making life less stressful. The outhouse in January was still the outhouse in January. The winter winds do not recognize blood quantum. Evidently I must have strong words with my mother's family about that negligent omission.

But in the years since I left the Reserve, and oddly enough more recently in my urban environment, there seems to be a peculiar attitude out there aimed at people like me and our not-so-distinctive situation. For the last decade or so, I have written quite extensively about life on the Reserve, the life of an Urban

Indian, and in some cases, my experiences as a person of mixed ancestry (though because of my childhood, my allegiance and consciousness is to my Ojibway heritage).

But like everyone, I had questions. I remember at one time, many years ago, running into Maria Campbell at a theatre opening party. Ironically, I was halfway through reading the book she had written with Linda Griffiths, *The Book Of Jessica*, about her own experiences writing a play about being Métis. I remember thinking it was providence that had guided her to this party, except in reality it was the director of the play. Often the two walk hand in hand.

After getting her to sign my copy of her book, I ended up telling her that occasionally, when I told people I was Native, they assumed I was Métis. So being still young and curious (I'm still curious but not so young), I naively asked her what was the difference between being a mixed blood and Métis.

The lovely and patient Ms. Campbell told me the Métis are a culture unto themselves. They have their own brand of music, style of dress, even a language of their own. And since I was raised on the Reserve by my mother and her family, also with a specific culture and language, and identified completely with that, to her I was essentially Ojibway, regardless of the melanin content of my skin. Needless to say, that cleared up a lot for me and answered a lot of questions. But unfortunately not everybody is as reasonable.

In more recent years, there seems to be a bizarre growing attitude of resentment towards that subject matter, and in some cases, my examination of the topic. One that reeks of potential internal racism within our community. And the irony is not lost on me. In the past, much like in the Black community, the lighter skinned Native people were more acceptable in the mainstream society than darker skinned people. And as a result, even within that marginalized culture, the lighter skins were favoured. Everybody wanted to look white. white was right.

"In the beginning, there was dark skin, and then God said let there be white... and it was good."

But today, with the advent of political correctness, the reverse is becoming the norm. The darker you are, the more acceptable you are. I knew a Native woman who refused to pursue a relationship with a half-breed friend of mine simply because she only wanted a full-blooded baby. Anything less was not acceptable. And I know other women who dated by the simple belief that the longer the braids and browner the eyes, the better.

Granted, there's a lot to be said for personal preference and having a cultural similarity to bond with. I personally prefer women with big screen televisions, but my point is that I have been lied to and misled. I am still waiting for that supposed easier existence in society that my friend in Curve Lake promised me, instead of what I have been experiencing up until now.

In reality, things have been getting harder the older I get. Not that long ago, I attended the launching of a documentary I directed on Native humour for the National Film Board. After the screening, there was a question and answer period where I revealed that two of the people featured in the documentary, Herbie Barnes and Don Kelly, were assisting me in writing a proposed television series I had pitched to the CBC.

Famed Aboriginal poet Michael Paul Martin raised his hand and commented that the three us were all half-breeds and he was curious if, because of that, we all shared some special connection and communication that allowed us to work so well together. For a moment I felt that our secret was out and our alien telepathy had been revealed, necessitating the postponement of our invasion. Instead I replied that if we get the series, we were going to give our production company a name based on the fact that the three of us were half-breeds. The company would be called... A Buck And a Half Productions.

The battle continues. Things have gotten to the point where, I'm told, my name is now officially a swear word or insult. Several months ago I received an email from the West Bay Reserve located on Manitoulin Island, from a gentleman whom this insult had been directed at. It seems he and a visual artist in that community have had difficulty in getting along, and for some reason, this visual artist had referred to this person in anger as that "Drew Hayden Taylor, half-breed, Métis wannabee."

Now somewhere along the journey of my life, my named joined the vernacular of Reserve cussing. If only I could get royalties. I guess I am now immortal. And I have no idea why or how this has happened. And specifically in this implication, I think there is a number of technical errors in reference to the term "Drew Hayden Taylor, half-breed, Métis wannabee." It's repetitious, inaccurate and a legitimate case of overkill. Oh well, I guess I should just be happy that I'm mentioned in conversation.

And perhaps one of the most outrageous examples I am personally familiar with came in the form of a letter to the editor. A gentleman named Paul Sayers had, rightly or wrongly, issues with an article I wrote for the Toronto magazine called *Now*. But more importantly, he had issues with me and he wasn't shy about demonstrating it.

Not only did he misspell my name in his letter but in reference to a book I wrote titled *Funny, You Don't Look Like One: Observations Of A Blue-Eyed Ojibway*, he concluded his critical letter by writing "P.S. Funny, I do look like one, tales from a proud BROWN-eyed Ojibway Man ." The strenuous capitalization was his. In the end, *Now Magazine* decided not to print the post-script because they felt it was uncomfortably close to being racist.

Now I can take criticism as much as the next person, I have a spot underneath the dresser where I frequently curl up into a fetal position, because I know no writer is perfect and not everybody agrees with the writer's opinion. But I'm not sure what my having blue-eyes has to with an article I wrote that had nothing to do with looking Native. The article was about a lack of professionalism exhibited by some Native organizations and people. Again, the irony was not lost on me.

In Bonita Lawrence's essay titled "Mixed-Race Urban

Native People: Surviving a Legacy of Policies of Genocide," she is quoted as saying "Most of the people I interviewed, however, did not have much sense of the extent of the daily privilege they enjoyed from having white skin...their concerns about not fitting in within the Native community at times appeared to overshadow their awareness of the fact that their lives were made much easier by the virtue of not looking Native." Again, I find it admirable that so many people know every single moment of my life as well as all my darker brothers and sisters. I must put a better lock on my diary.

Is the white looking drunk I see on the street any more fortunate than the Native looking one? And I realize the examples I have discussed here are small potatoes compared to the tragedies of Residential schools and other atrocities visited upon our Nations. But like most of my Native-looking family, I too am living in fear of diabetes. I am worried about and touched by the same issues any dark haired First Nations person, any place in Canada, might be.

And while I may not face those prejudices forced upon my darker skinned cousins, they do not have to face the reverse preconceptions people like I must deal with. It all evens out in the end.

It's a strange and weird world out there, even in this new Millennium. And as I'm told, I should be just breezing through life easier than my darker skinned brethren. I'll believe it when I no longer have to write articles like this.

JUNGLE BOY

The first eighteen years of my humble life were spent frolicking in the wilds of the Curve Lake First Nations, a small Ojibway community located in Central Ontario. It was a fairly happy existence where I climbed trees, played in the lakes and at the appropriate age, shocked to discover most of the girls on the Reserve were my cousins.

Then, as a struggling young writer intent on changing the world, I was also shocked to discover that my Reserve did not have a thriving film or theatre industry. So, citing those two reasons, it wasn't long before off I left, seeking my fortune in the big city. Since that fateful day when I spread my wings, I have found myself living almost constantly in an urban environment.

With that being said, it reminds me of a slightly augmented proverb: "You can take the boy out of the Rez, but you can't take the Rez out of the boy (or girl for those politically correct types)." Though I return home, practically every month for several days, the government and the Native community at large would no doubt classify me, officially, an "Urban Indian."

Yet, when I meet and talk with the real "Urban Indians," those born and raised in the city, it becomes quite obvious the slight differences in priorities and knowledge we share. I mean no disrespect to my more metropolitan brothers and sisters with whom I share good Thai restaurant and Martini bar locations, but the longer I live in the city, the more I become aware of the knowledge from my childhood – the stuff you think everybody would know – that occasionally bubbles to the surface.

For instance, a friend from the big city of Hamilton was visiting me in Curve Lake a few years back. I took her out for a walk that night, to show her the community. We found ourselves down by the lake, a dark and flat space in the quiet moonless night, when we heard a noise coming from the shoreline. I immediately recognized it as the throaty and haunting call of a bullfrog.

My friend cocked her head curiously and started walking towards the lake. I asked her where she was going, to which she replied "I want to go to this field and see the cows." I quickly explained the "field" and the "cows." After we stopped laughing, she defended her rural faux pas by exclaiming "What do I know, I'm a city Indian!"

Another time in Vancouver, an actress and I had finished work at a local theatre. We were walking down the street and she excitedly asked me if I wanted to see a part of town she called "the skids," an economically disadvantaged section of town where she grew up. I shook my head explaining I grew up on a Reserve, and that "urban decay doesn't really fascinate me." She laughed and said "oh yeah!"

Several years later, I visited this same woman, who had just recently been in another play of mine. In that play was a line about somebody cooking something called a chokecherry parfait for her character. A week after the production ended, we were back in Toronto where I found a chokecherry tree. I picked a handful and offered her some. As she ate them, she said "So these are chokecherries, where did you find them?"

"In your backyard." I took her out back and showed her the trees and the berries. She was fascinated.

Again, this is not a reflection or comment on any of my good friends. It's more or less one about myself. This land we call Turtle Island has many different types, kinds and varieties of Native people. And in the struggle to classify, for sake of argument, an "Urban" or "Rez" Indian, we forget to appreciate what ever we personally decide to classify ourselves. I've explored a lot of my own background as a mixed blood Native Canadian. However, I often forget I'm a mixed environment Native Canadian – half Rez, half Urban. I guess that makes me a Reban. I'm proud to say I know of both bullfrogs and Vietnamese cuisine. Chokecherries and how to buy a house in the big city. And most importantly, I accept the fact that life can be good, regardless of where you take your evening walks.

LIVING THE INDIGENOUS MYTH

Several years ago, my then Mohawk girlfriend and I, a fellow of proud Ojibway heritage, found ourselves in the history-rich halls of Europe, lecturing at a university deep in the heart of North-Eastern Germany. Our talk dealt with issues about being Native (or Red Indian as we were often referred to), the propaganda vs. the reality, how our two different Nations viewed life, just to mention just a few of the thousands of Aboriginal topics dis-cussed that day by an interested crowd.

Then this one young lady, a student at this former commu-nist University, put up her hand and asked a puzzling, though oddly naive question. It went something like "Do Indian women shave their legs and armpits like other North American women?" It was not the most anthropologically inquisitive ques-tion I have been asked, but unbeknownst to me the shaving of lower extremities and armpits in Europe is a largely unexplored area of female hygiene and evidently this topic warranted some investigation as to its Aboriginal application.

Other than the obvious follically oriented aspects of the question, it presented a rather obvious example of the same issue that also troubles our fair country known as Canada, thousands of miles away from that far off country in distance, language, culture but not that far in perception. I am referring to the myth, the number one myth in my perception, that permeates the col-lective North American unconscious (and conscious). The Myth of Pan-Indianism. As stated, this young German lady began her question with "Do Indian women...?" A common beginning for many Canadians, though First Nations, Native, Aboriginal, or Indigenous may be substituted for Indian. There is a persistent belief that we are all one people. These are obviously people who have never compared a Blood with a Naskapi.

Somebody with a lot of time on their hands once estimated that within the borders of what is now referred to as Canada, there were over fifty distinct and separate languages, and each distinct and separate language and dialect emerged from a distinct and separate culture. So, I began telling this woman, there is no answer to her question because technically, there is no "Indian/First Nations/Aboriginal..." nor could we speak for them all. To us there was only the Cree, the Ojibway, the Salish, the Innu, the Shuswap, etc.

I find myself explaining this concept annoyingly frequently, not just in Europe, but here in Canada – at The Second Cup, Chapters, the bus station. The power of that single myth is incredible. When people ask me or the government or God, "what do First Nations people want?" that's a tough question to answer (but then I can't speak for God). Some of the Micmac want to catch lobster, some of the Cree want to stop flooding and logging of their territory, the Mohawk want the right to promote their own language, and I know bingo is in there somewhere.

That is why every time I see a newspaper article or news report talking about the plight of the Aboriginal people, I find myself screaming at the offending method of communication. "Which People! Be specific!" That is why I never watch television in public.

That is the power of myths. By the very definition of that word, they are wrong and incorrect. That is why we as Native people (See, I do it myself) prefer not to use the term myth when referring to the stories of our ancestors, as in "The Myths and Legends of our People." There is just something inherently wrong about starting a traditional story with "This is one of the myths that was passed down from our Grandfathers...". Literally translated, it means "This is a lie that was handed down by our Grandfathers..."

The correct term preferred these days is teachings – as in "Our teachings say..." Its certainly more pleasant and accurate because it recognizes the fact that most myths exist for a purpose. Once you put aside the "lie" aspect, there is usually some nugget of metaphor or message within the subtext. And in the Native (there I go again!) way, we like to accentuate the positive and reject the negative.

However, the word legend can also be used instead of myth or teachings, provided you have oral permission from a recognized Elder, or written permission from an Aboriginal academic (any Nation will do), or the thumbs up from any Dene named Ted.

OTHER NATIVE-ORIENTED MYTHS INHERENT IN THE CANADIAN PSYCHE

It is believed by a good percentage of Canadians that there is a strong tradition of alcoholism existing within the Aboriginal population. I am reminded of another discussion I had, this time in Kenora, a decade or so ago. I was told that within a month's time, there had been almost 300 arrests of Aboriginals for alcohol-related offenses in that town. And Kenora's not that big a town. I was frightened for what that statistic told me... until it was explained that rather than the mind-boggling image of 300 drunken Indians running through the streets of Kenora, it just referred to the same dozen or two people who just got arrested over and over and over again. It's all in how you read the statistic. And nobody told me how many white people had been arrested for similar offenses.

And while acknowledging that certain communities do indeed suffer from substance abuse problems, (like many non-Native communities I might add), I can safely say that neither myself, my mother, my best friend and most of the other people of some form of Aboriginal descent I consider friends and acquaintances, are alcoholics, it makes me wonder why this myth is so persuasive.

It is also believed by a good percentage of Canadians that all Native people are poor. Unfortunately, many communities do suffer from mind-numbing poverty, as do many non-Native communities. But again, contrary to popular belief, capitalism was not a foreign concept to Canada's earliest inhabitants. There were levels of wealth and status back then, and that tradition with all its good and bad aspects persist to this day, except instead of counting your horses, today they might count their horse-power.

Several weeks ago, there was an editorial in a Toronto paper attacking a rumour about a coalition of Aboriginal people that had expressed an interest in buying the Ottawa Senators. The columnist thought the idea preposterous because "these are the same people who can't afford to pay tax on a pack of smokes; the same people who are so poor they claim government policy is forcing them to live in neighbourhoods where a rusted car with more than one flat tire is considered a lawn ornament."

That is a myth. The ratio of rusted car on lawn to no rusted car on lawn is so disproportionate, its not even worth mentioning. And yes, there are some wealthy Native people out there. I wish I knew more of them personally but I know they are out there and they exist. But again, it's a hard concept to believe when the media only features the desperate, the tragic and the sad. A financially secure First Nations person should not be considered an oxymoron.

Conclusion:

I was asked to write an essay on the "myths of a common "Indian Identity." So basically, I was asked to comment on lies about something that doesn't exist. That sounds more like politics to me.

And if you're still curious about whether Indian women shave their legs and armpits... you'll have to ask a woman because it's an arcane secret, conceived in antiquity and relegated to the chosen wise few.

WE DESERVE OUR OWN ETHNIC HOLIDAY TOO!

Hot on the heels of this year's St. Patrick's Day festivities, it occurred to me that we, as Native people, not only are lacking our own special day of celebration, but in fact, I think we should demand one. We want the same cultural, day-to-party, equality!

Yes, I know we have First Nations Day in late June but realistically, First Nations Day sounds too much like a political holiday. It lacks the ring of celebratory fun and excess that we've learned to love in St. Patrick's Day. And I happen to know, for a fact (and I can swear to this in court if you want), that Native people like to party and celebrate their culture as much as, if not more than, the Irish. And Heaven help those who are both Irish and Native. The potato stories they must swap...

If you scan the calendar, there are many holidays set aside specifically for the various ethnic and cultural races across the world. For instance, there are several Jewish holidays (Yom Kippur and Hanukkah to name a few), Afro-American (Martin Luther King Jr. Day in the States), numerous Catholic and other Christian days of celebration (Christmas and Easter), a day for Pilgrims (Thanksgiving), and even a holiday for British Monarchs (Victoria Day), but no real day for Aboriginal partying. And I'm fairly certain there are more Native people in the world than Pilgrims.

That is why I believe we should start a movement to rename First Nations Day and remove the political and boring stigma attached to it. We need something fun and catchy that matches the Native spirit. Keeping with the spirit of St. Patrick's Day, I suggest we call it Ste. Marie Day in honour of Buffy Ste. Marie, that lovable Cree songstress. I'm sure she's a party girl, and the

114

similarity in Saint–related names wouldn't hurt to keep up the Irish connection. We're talking a theme here.

St. Patrick was famous for driving all the snakes out of Ireland, thus one of the reasons for all the celebrations. Personally, not being Irish, I've got nothing against snakes (that's probably one of those Catholic things) but I am a firm believer in any excuse for a party. With Ste. Marie Day, we could say Ste. Marie drove John Kim Bell up the wall (for everybody who isn't aware of Buffy and the Aboriginal Achievement Awards controversy a few years back, shame on you. You're missing a good story).

While I hope we could keep all the drunkenness and mayhem down to a dull roar, I do, however, trust we can infuse Ste. Marie Day with the same amount of enthusiasm and tradition normally associated with St. Patrick's Day. Think of it as a pow wow on steroids. On second thought, don't.

Ste. Marie Day. Doesn't it just want to make you rush out and drink a keg of beer? Except it wouldn't be green beer, it would be red beer. And instead of singing Celtic tunes from the Old Country (which is odd considering Turtle Island is as old if not older than the "Old Country"), we would be singing Kashtin tunes all day. Picture yourself at a Ste. Marie Day party, sitting around the campfire, everybody singing out in unison, choruses of "Uitshi," followed by a rousing version of "Pakuakumit," the evening sprinkled with the odd Buffy tune for continuity. It's enough to make both you and your bow quiver.

Instead of a shamrock, we could all wear hats with little sweetgrass braids flopping back and forth. Of course, red would be the colour of the day. We have little people too that we can capitalize and merchandise. And perhaps most fabulous of all, everybody on the streets, both Native and non-Native, would be faking bad Indian accents as they wish each other a great Ste. Marie Day. "Try not to have too much fun on Ste. Marie's Day, 'kay? We got too many t'ings to do tomorrow, eh?"

What does First Nations Day offer? A free day off work for all the Native organizations. Big deal. That's what sick days are for. I rest my case. If anybody wants me, I'll be planning the parade routes.

CULTURE BY ASSOCIATION

Not long ago, I read in a Native newspaper, a brief biography of someone I have known for going on two decades now. For most of those two decades, this Torontonian had identified herself as being white, with a mild interest in Native issues. More recently, I was surprised to learn that since she married a Native gentleman, and had a child by him, she was now referring to herself specifically as an *Anishnawbe-qua*, an Ojibway woman. Suddenly out of nowhere, she had a completely different ancestry.

You know, you hear in the news all the time about scientists experimenting with gene and DNA swapping, but you never think it will come into your own neck of the woods. Or maybe I just shouldn't have taken her to that Billy Jack Film Festival in the 80's. Or that damned *Dances With Wolves* film again!

Seriously, this is a delicate topic to explore, one that could get me in a lot of trouble, depending on who reads this and where they stand in the minefield I call "spousal cultural appropriation," otherwise known as SCA. I refer, of course, to individuals who have married people of the Aboriginal persuasion, and now repeatedly identify themselves as having the same status (no pun intended) in that same community.

In many cases, this practice is referred to rather vividly as being "Indian by ejaculation." God knows I've done my share of passing out citizenship but it sure beats the hell out of all the Bill C–31 paperwork and that pesky lineage requirement.

And to be fair to the other sex, I know of a similar case in Six Nations involving an Iroquois woman who took her non-Native husband to several clan mothers in a desperate attempt to get him adopted into one of the Nations. Eventually she was successful and he now successfully identifies with one of those Nations.

Technically this is not all that new an idea. Marrying somebody for their nationality has been an age-old immigration scam for years. I was once asked, by a friend, to marry a woman from Czechoslovakia so she could become Canadian. Needless to say, I didn't jump at the chance or I'd be writing this from jail.

But of the women I have been lucky enough to date over the years, and those exceptional ones I ended up having special relationships with, I can't help wondering if my "familiarity" with them makes me a member of the Filipino, Irish, Delaware, Cree, Puerto Rican, Micmac... (and this was just my Vegas vacation last year) nation and a proud representative of their culture?

More recently, I had an excellent relationship with a marvelous Mohawk woman and though I have great respect and honour for her people and culture, I never felt the urge to "become" Mohawk. My lacrosse skills are just not up to it yet. So that's what puzzles me about the SCA issue. At no time during my current or past relationships, did the thought of ever wanting to call myself a Mohawk man, Filipino man, or the host of other cultures I was privileged to briefly be exposed to, occur. Granted I have a Métis belt, a Micmac sweater and a Salish painting, but I drew the line there.

I don't believe it's like becoming Jewish where you can take certain classes, get something snipped off, and then convert, and finally be legitimately called a Jew. I am curious at what it currently takes for a non-Native to call themselves a Native person. Must you take Ojibway 101? Show a marked preference for French braiding your hair? Learn how to kill a deer with a corkscrew? Make bannock with your elbows? Maybe we've allowed it to be too easy to join the Aboriginal bandwagon. Perhaps if we snipped something off, the interest might wane.

In the end, I am somewhat mystified by this constant fascination and obsession many non-Natives feel towards our culture. I just find it a little odd and slightly annoying that thousands of years of culture and tradition can be appropriated for the cost of a marriage license (if that).

Perhaps its the fact we have one of the highest suicide rates in the civilized world (and I do use that term loosely). Maybe its the fact our life expectancy rate is substantially lower than the National average. Could it be the constant turmoil with the various levels of government over land claims, hunting/fishing rights, reparations, etc. Possibly its that the standards of living on most Reserves are a national disgrace. Conceivably its the fact that in the next thirty years, of the over fifty Aboriginal languages once spoken in this country, its estimated only three will be left – for possibly another thirty or forty years.

But hey, we got cool hair and funky pow wows.

LET ME TELL YOU ABOUT MY FRIENDS AND FAMILY
(Be Afraid... Be Very Afraid!)

IT ALL STARTED WITH A CAT...

Some time back my ex-girlfriend, Dawn, and I decided to get a kitten. She had never had one in her life and I thought the raising of a kitten together would be something fun to do. As many new pet owners often do, we were stumped for an adequate name. We wanted it to be a wonderful and magnificent title, worthy of a pet of ours. But nothing immediately came to mind.

In a moment of genius, Dawn suggested I ask my mother, who is fluent in Ojibway, for an Ojibway name befitting it's adopted Aboriginal heritage. On the phone from the Reserve, my mother paused for a moment in thought before offering up her double-edged suggestion.

"You should call it *Oh-shan*" she innocently recommended. Admittedly, my Ojibway is much rustier than it should be and I was momentarily perplexed by the phrase and couldn't come up with an English translation. So I asked my mother what *Oh-shan* meant and with out a beat (which makes me believe she was waiting for me to ask) she announced "It means grandchild because that's probably as close as I'll ever get to being a grandparent!"

Me thinks my mother may have had an alternate agenda than just the naming of a cat. With me being the ripe age of thirty-nine, I think my mother may have a few concerns in that area and wanted to share them. So much for just wanting a name for a cat. And to complicate the matter, Dawn was beginning to make nesting noises in that general area too, and I was beginning to feel like the Germans caught between the Allies and the Russians.

It's not that I have anything against children, it's just that I'm a single child of a single parent and I was never privy to the

122

instructions manual on the care and feeding of said creatures.

While on the other hand, Dawn is one of four children and has had some experience teaching Kindergarten. She is somewhat more qualified than I.

All I dimly remember is my aunts mumbling something about burping, peeing and the high cost of kid's sneakers. I think they need to seriously rewrite the promotional campaign. And many of those same aunts have told me that I'm still a kid at heart, but I tend to discount that statement because over the years I've found that most women say that about their men anyways.

So what to do? What to do? I tried telling Dawn and my mother that we have three plants that require looking after, but they didn't seem to buy it. I find it important to add at this moment that Dawn was famous for not watering my plants while I was traveling and yet SHE'S the one who wanted children! I refuse to be the only one watering the kids.

And to make the situation slightly more embarrassing, I have a cousin that's two days older than me, and already he's a GRANDFATHER! All our lives we were somewhat competitive and I guess he finally topped me. Every time I go home, I can see it in all my relation's eyes "What have you been doing with your life?" It's an accepted statistic in the Native community that 50% of the Aboriginal population out there is under twenty-five years old. Evidently I'm not holding up my end of the Status card.

So after pondering the increasingly less philosophic and increasingly persistent question of "what to do?". I finally came up with an answer for Dawn. I told her that I would be more than delighted to have a) a child, b) children, provided she can assure me that they would, in no way, interfere with my accepted and comfortable writing schedule.

I don't quite understand why she burst out laughing.

WHAT WOULD HAPPEN IF THE CIGAR STORE INDIAN DIDN'T HAVE ANY CIGARS?

I am very proud of my mother – actually for a number of reasons including important issues like managing to raise a child as a single parent on the Reserve, etc. But more recently, I am so very proud of my mother for the simple fact that, at the age of sixty-eight, she has decided to stop smoking. After lighting up as long as I can remember (she won't even tell me how old she was when she started), my mother is a free, non-addicted woman! Way to go mom!

But the thing that astounds me is that because she is sixty-eight years old and obviously rather advanced in life, she has been told, even urged by several people (who shall remain nameless should I ever return home again in peace) that quitting smoking isn't worth her time. "You're almost seventy," she was told by one person, "why quit now?" Evidently these people believe old dogs can't learn new tricks, or there's no use crying over spilled milk, or leopards can't change their spots, or you shouldn't provide the opportunity to let a writer include as many cliche's in a sentence as possible to help reinforce his mother's determination.

Regardless of these non-supportive people, my mother has resisted the temptation and remains non-combustible to this day, several months later. And as luck and irony would have it, it wasn't much later that I came across a laminated poster on a dusty wall located in a youth centre on Manitoulin Island. In bold letters it read "Tobacco is sacred. Don't Abuse it." And more than ever, it struck home.

There always was and still is a strong connection between tobacco and Native people. First cultivated by North Americans

124

untold centuries ago, it has always been used in our ceremonies and rituals. It is, perhaps, the most important of the four sacred herbs – the others being cedar, sage and sweetgrass. Tobacco is normally used in pipe ceremonies so that the smoke would carry the dreams and prayers up into the sky where the Creator dwelled. Being a Pipe Carrier is a position of great respect. Or sometimes tobacco is just put down on or in the Earth as a thank you or a gift to Mother Earth. Regardless, tobacco has long been a respected part of our heritage.

But times change and with them, heritage too, it seems. People who smoke a pack or two every day, must have a lot of prayers (Please God, don't let me get cancer) to give. Now a days, most Native people use tobacco, not in sacred ceremonies, but as a way of placating an addiction. First Nations people have one of the highest smoking rates (let's not forget its kin, chewing tobacco) in the developed world. What once was used sparingly and respectfully, is now simply a habit. An especially dangerous habit with all the non-Native chemicals and additives currently available in every cigarette.

To make things worse, I have even heard people rationalize this abuse by saying "Native people have always smoked. It's part of our culture." Well, so was getting up at dawn, riding a horse bareback, and eating turtle eggs raw. Ask them the last time they did any of those on a regular basis?

And if we were to take this questionable and misguided argument to its logical conclusion, the Aboriginal people of Peru and Columbia once chewed the leaves of a small plant called the coca plant. It helped alleviate the symptoms of altitude sickness and would sometimes act as a pick-me-up during the long treks through the mountains. So does that mean the Indigenous people of the Andes are all cocaine and crack addicts because it is part of their culture and heritage? If it is, that's news to me and I'm sure to the noble descendants of the Incas.

Continuing this train of thought, the Catholic church uses wine as a sacrament during Holy Communion, as the blood of Christ. Does that mean all Catholics are alcoholics (I wouldn't touch that line with a ten foot pole) and vampires? Jeez, and to think I almost married one.

I don't think I'm going out on a limb here by saying that smoking, as done today, was not part of our culture. Cigarettes are not absolution. The Creator does not use chewing tobacco. Emphysema is not a blessing.

YOU CAN'T RETURN HOME AGAIN

Growing up on the Curve Lake Reserve located somewhere in the deepest, darkest part of tourist Ontario, I enjoyed a certain amount of social and cultural familiarity. Knowing that within those artificial walls created by the Department of Indian Affairs, I could expect life to change very little. Living on a Reserve was, in many ways, an oasis against momentary trends, fads and other patterns of a fickle society. In fact, and I say this with great appreciation, those Reserve walls protected and insulated me during the disco and punk rock eras. I was spared the perils of polyester leisure suits.

As often as possible I return home to the land where I was born, to visit family, recharge my batteries, and generally remind myself where my stories come from. And for many of those years I have been away, little has changed in my home. I used to believe, paraphrasing an old saying, that "only death, taxes and Curve Lake are eternal."

But the more I go home these days, the more I can see the steady, encroaching fingerprints of Canadian society making their way in the bosom of my beloved community. It's akin to an alien invasion– a bureaucratic one – the completion of one started over five hundred years ago. And I am afraid. Very afraid.

These days, the streets of Curve Lake echo with an unfamiliar influence. First of all, the streets of Curve Lake now all have official names. with signs and everything. When I was growing up, we all knew where somebody lived, so the need for street signs seemed unnecessary, even silly. I mean, if you didn't know where you lived, or your cousin or uncle, you were a pretty sad individual.

And perhaps there was some personal pride in the fact that

127

if anybody from off the Reserve made their way into our humble community, they would find themselves helpless and probably lost, with nothing but the stars and sun to guide them. Ancient Iroquoians used to build huge walled stockades around their communities which included an elaborate maze near the front gate so intruders and hostile parties would hopefully get lost long enough for the inhabitants of the village to mount a defense. Not naming our streets was the Ojibway method of doing this.

But now this little Ojibway community is crisscrossed with streets named Weequod, Whetung, Mississauga, and Lonely Pine (which was cut down recently making the street name somewhat moot).

Not only are the streets now named, but heaven forbid the government has seen fit to give each individual house its own number! Unfortunately (though it pains me to say it) there is a certain amount of logic to it – this way emergency vehicles can find the right street and the right house rather than relying on local directions – "Take a right at the pine tree, go over the ditch and then through the sumach and you'll find Fred's. And Say hello for me."

Another fond childhood memory deals with recollections of dogs running free, playing, cavorting, being one with the land. But that is no more. New bylaws by the village have now made it illegal to let your dogs run free. They must be registered and tied up at all times. But I think "what's the point of being a dog on the Reserve then?" The last time I was home, I saw dozens of dogs now chained to trees and stakes, doomed to spend the rest of their lives in a ten foot circle. This is not the Reserve I knew and loved. It's now like living in a small non-Native town! I knew we were in trouble the day we could get pizza delivery in the village.

But, as always, there are certain things that still remind you that things will always remain the same no matter what. Just a few months ago, local residents in one part of the village were requesting speed bumps on some of the subdivision roads to deter fast drivers from hitting children. Through some bureau-cratic mix-up, the speed bumps were installed without proper authorization. And they were placed too close to the various cor-ners, so they had to be dug up and removed. There are now depressions in the pavement showing where the bumps used to be. I'm told the depressions are now just as good a deterrent as the speed bumps. Things like this still remind me that I'm home.

Luckily, there are a few universalities that still exist now, and no doubt will continue to exist long after the hype over the Y2K bug. I speak of course of denim (as versatile and ubiqui-tous as buckskin used to be), plaid (where Scottish styles go to die) and country music (where everything goes to die). At least these will allow me to retain my sanity.

Though, I hear, there is talk of a subway line...

A ROCK AND A HARD PLACE

My mother used to tell me that when she was young, her parents used to keep her in line by saying that if she wasn't a good girl, the *"Nodwag"* would come and take her away. Roughly translated *"Nodwag"* meant the Mohawks. Evidently this was a fairly common practice in my Annishnawbe community. It seems the Mohawk nation was on the same par with the "bogeyman" and decades ago naughty Ojibway children huddled under their blankets in fear of being taken away by these horrible *"Nodwag."*

This is no doubt an after effect of the rivalry between both Nations dating back to the fur trade when the Ojibway and Mohawks fought it out. This was a war instigated by the English and French for the lucrative beaver pelts and other assorted goodies the Europeans wanted and got other people to collect. At times, this trade war got brutal and evidently, some generations are still having to deal with it.

That being understood, sixty years later, my mother's worst fear had come true. Her son, a very good boy, was indeed taken away by the dreaded *"Nodwag."* Only this time the bogeyman came in the shape of a beautiful Mohawk woman who I must admit, kidnapped me quite willingly. No kicking and screaming here!

Flying in the face of the concept of pan-Indianism, the unique collaboration of our two different societies presented some interesting and unique inter-cultural relations. Often times we sat around discussing our various upbringings, cultural baggage, and generally trying to make sense of our distinctive bonding and what ever synthesis might occur from it. See what happens when you don't have cable.

For instance, I am half Ojibway and half Caucasian (of no definable nation), which as I've often said, makes me an Occasion. She on the other hand, was half Irish and half Mohawk, which in turn made her an Irawk (or better known to car lovers – an Iroc). So, we came to the conclusion that if or when we ever had kids, they would be full blooded half-breeds-Ojihawks I guess or in combining our traditional names for ourselves, Ohwe-naabe.

But there seemed to be a constant, though never acknowledged, contest of cultures – a sort of ideological battle of the Nations. On my part, I had begun, what I call, the slow, subtle "Ojibwification" of this Mohawk woman. Without her being aware, I tried to seduce and introduce her subconscious to the wonderful and complex world of the Ojibway. My success was proven by the fact she can say, in Ojibway, that someone has a "nice behind." Though how she came up with that particular phrase escapes me.

On her part though, when upset, she had that familiar Mohawk tendency to blockade the bathroom, where as I, as an Ojibway, just beaded something. Also, during that time, I ate more corn, beans and squash (the notorious Iroquois Three Sisters – once the staple of their diet) than I ever had. And for some strange reason, I occasionally felt the need to play lacrosse. Then, finally, another strange occurrence, I too seemed to know how to say "nice behind" in Mohawk. But other than that, I had resisted her psychological brainwashing.

Except on a more domestic and culturally non-specific front. There, the battle has taken on a more unusual turn. As an Ojibway, my people were hunter/gatherers, nomads that followed the moose and deer, building temporary homes for the seasons then moving on, as the need arose. Dawn's Nation, the Mohawk of the Iroquois Confederacy, erected whole villages and permanent settlements. They were an agricultural people who had to remain fixed to tend their corn, beans and squash.

I have spent most of my adult life moving from apartment to apartment, quite contently moving from job or contract as the opportunity was necessary. No doubt a genetic residue handed down over the millenniums. Dawn, on the other hand, wanted a house. There was no mention of a garden for the three sisters,but she wanted a permanent place to call home. Evidently my wandering days were over.

This became one of the more recent Ojibway/Mohawk battles of history. I lost. So we purchased a house together and took up housekeeping. I was allowed to roam the backyard though.

I am not sure if this is a cultural quirk, or a personal one for her. But until we met, and moved in together, I had not been aware that the entire world, both Native and non-Native, revolves around the simple fact that in order for the Universe and existence as we know it to continue, all towels in the bathroom must match. And each bathroom must have a different set of coloured bath towels. The joke is... this is not a joke. For if this rule is not maintained and upheld, reality as we know it might end and civilization might perish.

I say this because there were sparks aplenty the time we went shopping and lo, I almost brought down heaven and earth by mis-categorizing a set of towels she was considering purchasing. She innocently held up a pale looking towel from a whole row of pale looking towels and asked "what do you think of this colour?" I stupidly replied with the truth, "What colour? It's white." Her response was enough to make you think the Fifth Horseman of the Apocalypse was an interior decorator.

"It's not white," she said coldly. I proceeded to get my first lecture on the spectrum of white towel purchasing. It seems white isn't white, it could be bone, ivory, cream, or simply off-white to name just a few options. It was scary. There's that famous saying the Inuit have twenty-three names for snow. The same number probably exists for white towels.

Thirty seven years on this planet, almost twenty as a journalist and writer, having travelled to almost a dozen countries around the world, and somehow this was a missing element in my education. All towels in the bathroom must match. And white isn't necessarily white. The more I learn, the more I realize I have to learn. I wonder if Descartes and Einstein knew this towel thing.

Somewhere deep down inside, it makes me wonder if the whole Ojibway/Mohawk rivalry that happened centuries ago had, maybe, something to do with the beaver pelts not matching properly.

Now, I'm told, if I can just learn how to fold them properly...

BOY IS MY FACE RED!

Okay the author admits it. He has been somewhat humbled. Somewhat deflated by his experiences at the Mississauga's of Scugog First Nations in Ontario. Drew Hayden Taylor... big time playwright/journalist/ writer for television/filmmaker etc... winner of several prestigious writing awards and author of eleven pretty good books... a forgotten presence in a room where he was supposed to be selling some of his books and signing autographs to his adoring public.

Instead, he sat at the end of the room. Surrounded by his untouched books and unused pen. Alone. Looking at all the people at the other end of the room, flocking to and purchasing calendars from the beautiful lady he could occasionally catch glimpses of, between the constant waves of fans that would engulf her – her pen working feverishly as she signed her name, Dawn T. Maracle.

Part of him was happy that this woman was having such a successful time selling calendars, since he lived with her at the time. He remembers how proud he was that she had completed the first year of her Ph. D in Native Education, and for being the first Mohawk Cheerleader in the Toronto Argos history (though she is now with the Tiger Cats – evidently Cheerleaders can be traded too). Quite a unique combination – a Mohawk, Ph.D cheerleader – the author has often thought to himself "There's a play in there somewhere but people would think I made it up." He smiled, happy for her. Then he remembered how lonely his side of the room was.

The calendar she was selling is adorned by beautiful women in bathing suits. It was the Argos Swimsuit calendar and she was Miss February and was by far the prettiest. And everybody wanted a signed copy, including several women. The author was puzzled because the year was half over, yet all these people still wanted the 2001 calendars for some strange, mysterious reason. One Chief said he was only buying it because the proceeds went to charity. "This is for the kids" he said. Uh huh.

She was a celebrity here and he was worrying if there was enough ink in her pen to please all her admiring fans. The author rearranged his books yet again, in another futile attempt to lure potential customers. And again, the author thought to himself how hard it is to compete with bikinis. He marveled at it's reflection of today's society – how people don't read anymore, they would simply prefer to look at pictures instead. Then he remembered he had three of those calendars himself. And way too many unsold books.

He spotted two uncles and an aunt in the crowd orbiting the far end of the table. He made a silent note to himself, "No Christmas Card for them this year. And with all the calendars it looks like they've boughten, they sure won't be able to forget when December 25th arrives."

The author leaned back in his chair, giving up all hope of recognition and sales. With his keen, analytical mind, he tried to come up with a way to prevent this embarrassing incident from every happening again. One idea he came up with is to never come to Scugog again, but he surmises quickly it's probably not a Scugog-specific problem.

He could petition Parliament to ban and outlaw all calendars. He wondered if it's legally possible to put a restraining order on anything that marks the passing days. But he derived some small solace from the fact that in six months, the calendar would be obsolete and things would return to normal.

Thinking optimistically, he envisioned selling a book before Christmas. Then tragedy strikes. The Mohawk Ph.D cheerleader informed the author that the Tiger Cats are thinking of putting out a calendar for the 2002 season. The author ponders whether it's worth having those two new books published the next year.

Maybe he should just learn how to say "Would you like fries with that?" and embrace a new career.

He started to put his books away into a box, along with his tarnished and deflated ego. The author managed to catch a glimpse of the Mohawk Ph.D cheerleader signing yet another calendar when he gets his fabulous idea. It is truly great and glorious. He kicks himself for not seeing the obvious. Fight fire with fire he reasoned! On the cover of his next book, he himself will appear in a bikini and no doubt sales will double, triple even!

He smiled secretly to himself. He will be ready, come the new year. And she will be in serious trouble.

CHRISTMAS TREASURES

So Christmas has come and gone and all that's left is the turkey soup (the official post-Christmas meal, sort of the Yuletide hang-over soup) as well as the three or four extra pounds riding shot-gun along your waist making those new Christmas pants a questionable option. And the question of the week is... was it worth all the hassle and family confusion? Was Santa nice to you this year or were you a bad boy or girl and somebody forgot to tell you?

Of course I can only speak for myself but I returned home to the Reserve this Christmas full of the usual holiday misgivings; which cousin will I be mistaken for this time, how many times will I be told that "a big time writer like you should dress better. And get a haircut," or my favorite, "don't you have a real job yet?" Yes, I am truly home.

And of course like everywhere in the Universe, even on Canadian Reserves, the immutable laws of Christmas are still honoured and respected. I, along with many other non-Natives, Asians, Blacks, and every other culture and cultures spread around the world, received a stunningly inordinate supply of socks and underwear. I'm talking a lot! I'm not kidding about this, but I actually don't think I've ever personally bought a pair of socks or underwear in my life. My Christmas bonanza gets me through the entire year with the odd sweat sock to spare.

With my mother being the oldest of fourteen, and as a result, making me one of over sixty cousins (on a good night), it has now become the family motto that when in doubt, buy Drew socks and underwear. I now get Christmas cards from the Hudson's Bay, thanks to my family. Maybe that's part of the plan to make me dress better.

So this week I begin my annual New Year's tradition of retiring some of my older, more well-used socks and underwear. It's like parting with old friends. It seems a shame to throw out what seems to be perfectly good, broken in, comfy undergarments, but what other option is there? Who do you know that would want previously owned socks and underwear? Perhaps the question should be, would you want to know someone who would want previously owned underwear and socks? I'm sure there's probably even a website for it somewhere, but I don't think I'm that interested in finding it.

Luckily I did get a few more presents than just the previously mentioned socks and underwear. But as usual, it was the presents I had given my girlfriend that year that provoked the most discussion. She seemed a little perturbed with some of the more functional gifts I gave her. "Some of my friends got jewellery. You never give me jewellery." After years of living together, I somehow managed to detect a subtle hint.

I tried to explain to her that we, as a couple, had progressed far beyond the materialistic stage. We had, in fact, advanced past that capitalistic phase and were now enjoying the more spiritual, emotional plane in our relationship. We were into the good stuff now. For some reason, that didn't seem to impress her much.

Maybe I shouldn't have given her my extra socks and underwear.

USING A LITTLE MUSCLE

About three and a half years ago, I was doing a reading/lecture in, of all places, a college in North Bay Ontario. I do a lot of readings. It comes with being an author (and the simple fact that I have a hungry mortgage to feed). About a week later I saw a photograph of myself at that reading, in a Native newspaper. That lone photograph ended up being perhaps one of the most expensive and painful things to happen in my life (except for one ex-girlfriend but I won't get into that right now; that's a whole different column).

In that picture I was standing, reading from one of my books. It was a side shot, sort of a three/quarters body profile. It was also the first time I seriously noticed that I had a belly. I mean a serious belly. A serious, serious, serious belly. I knew I was no longer the svelte boy who worked his way through college as a 168 lb. security/bouncer type person in a school pub full of substantially more well fed football players. That too is another column.

But I had a belly. And jowls. I looked like my uncles. Not that I have anything against my uncles, but it just suddenly hit me that I was developing that familiar Ojibway deer gut (without the benefit of deer!) I was terrified that maybe, in keeping with the contemporary Ojibway male body progression, my legs were getting shorter and skinnier as my top half got larger. Like a mushroom. You've heard the term "scared straight?" Thus was born "scared skinny."

That single picture made me realize I had a serious choice to make. Keep watching all the television I want between meals of neckbones, baloney sandwiches and vats of coke (the soft drink – I don't think there are too many chubby drug addicts out

139

there). Add to that the high rate of diabetes in my immediate family and I knew something should be... had to be done. So on that fateful day, I decided to join a gym.

Oh I'd joined gyms before, two or three times but for some reason, I just never stuck with it. One time I paid for six months membership and never went once. I didn't have the motivation. Well, somewhere in the wilds of North Bay is a film negative that became my motivation.

Unlike my first forays into the world of calorie burning and groaning, I figured I'd better do this right. All those nights of watching television (between those neckbone and coke snacks of course), I kept hearing about movie stars hiring personal trainers. Everybody who's anybody was doing it and I definitely wanted to be a somebody. I figured I've written for television. I should have the right to hire a personal trainer.

Word of caution: they are expensive. But they can be worth it. I figure the amount of money I saved from buying neckbones and baloney, would more than offset the cost of a personal trainer. So I learned the correct way to do everything. Even eat. I got to go from my usual two meals a day up to five! Gotta love these personal trainers. Unfortunately, neckbones and coke weren't on their recommended diets. But the long and short of it is, I have stuck with it to this day. I lost almost twenty pounds just from the cardio machine itself, but the irony is I put it all back on from the weight training. I'm almost the exact same weight as when I started.

As an avid gym-going Indian, it has provided me with some unexpected adventures. With the amount of readings I do all over the place, I find myself in many different parts of the world (though I haven't been back to North Bay since – too many bad memories I guess). You will never know the pain of wandering the streets of Whitehorse looking for an open health club on a wintery Sunday. Or calling clubs in Penticton that take walk in's. Basically I can claim to have bench pressed from Happy Valley, Labrador, to Prince Rupert, British Columbia.

But I also found out it's difficult to pump iron in Germany

or Italy or so I 've discovered. Either they don't have gyms, or they hide them, or something. How Swartzeneggar got the way he is I'll never know. In Venice I contemplated swimming a few of the canals but upon seeing them and discovering it might be easier to jog them. I thought I'd just rather get fat on great pasta.

However, I've noticed some unusual things while working out. I like to kill two birds with one stone when I can, (as long as the birds are lean and throwing the stone can give you a great lat and delt workout) so when in most gyms, I put on my social anthropologist jock strap and watch my fellow enthusiasts. The first thing you notice is that as a sport or leisure activity, working out is one of the most narcissistic activities you can find. Everybody there is trying to stay thin, look good, get toned. There's very little slumming in health clubs.

To prove this, you will notice all health clubs are lined with mirrors. Floor to ceiling, wall to wall, shiny mirrors for everybody to look at themselves. I've seen men and women checking out their abs, their biceps for several minutes at a time. A few short years ago, I couldn't help checking out my stomach, except that I was watching television at the time. I had to look over it to see the screen. Sometimes I used to shift it off to the left for a better view.

And there's that myth about health clubs being a great place to pick up chicks (or guys), since everybody is in tight or revealing clothes and supposedly looking good. Not true. If there is a time in my life that I do not feel like picking somebody up (and this is keeping in mind that under no circumstances would I ever consider trying to pick somebody up, gym or no gym, no matter what anybody might tell whoever I'm dating), it is when I am in the gym. I am sweaty, tired, making unattractive faces with every weight I lift, grunting uncontrollably. Yeah, sure makes me hot.

I also have many female friends who work out and they tell me what a nuisance it is when guys come over under the guise of offering to help them work out, or teach them a new technique (yeah, we've all heard that before), when in reality, they're just checking them out. It's gotten to the point where I'm afraid of even casually glancing at any woman who might be in the weight room for fear of becoming a cliché.

But this one time I did happen to accidentally glance at a girl in the gym, I remember in admiration, saying to myself, "She's really hot. Check out the delts on her. They're so nice and big. I wonder if they're real." It was then I realized I'd probably been working out too much.

It says a lot about our North American culture. We actually pay people to go some place and work out. Where in developing countries, people beg to be paid for work. What would our grand mothers and grandfathers think of wasting so much time, lifting weights, running on treadmills, expending all this energy that creates little and accomplishes nothing other than looking good. They would probably just shake their heads.

It reminds me of a quote from George Bernard Shaw. I don't remember it exactly but it goes something like this: "When I die, I want to be all used up. I don't want to think that I had anything left to waste."

Another quote comes to mind. "Live fast. Die young. Leave behind a good looking corpse." I don't know who said that but I disagree. I think there's got to be a middle ground between the two. Maybe someday I'll find it.

Perhaps it has something to do with putting a plate of neck-bones on a small table in front of a treadmill. Beats the hell out of dangling a carrot.

EVIDENTLY I'VE BEEN A GOOD BOY

As many reputable philosophers have urged, every once in a while a person should step back, take a good look at their life and figure out where they fit on the big bingo card of Creation. Always remember, the center square comes free, but everything else is your responsibility, though I'm not quite sure Socrates or Satre ever quite phrased it that way.

The reason I bring this up is that on some days, I wake up and realize I must be living somebody else's life. I mean I grew up thinking I would probably spend most of my adult life working at my Band Office, embezzling money from Indian Affairs Canada. Alas, that glorious career was denied to me. Instead. I find myself doing things and going places no self respecting boy from the Rez should find himself doing or being, let alone dreaming.

For instance, I just recently returned from a trip to Venice, Italy where I lectured on Native theatre in Canada, my eleventh book comes out this fall, and I'm buying a new house with my *buz'gem* (Ojibway for person who steals all the blankets when she's not busy telling you to wash them in the next load of laundry). And perhaps the most amazing thing of all, (and we're talking some serious mind boggling here) is that my already–mentioned *buz'gem* is a professional cheerleader for the Toronto Argos football team! I'm not kidding. May Matthew Coon Comb eat my status card if I'm lying.

I repeat... I'm living with a cheerleader, outfit and all. I seem to remember asking Santa for this back in my adolescent years, but it's not something you would expect him to come through on. Santa may be slow but never count him out.

On top of that, it seems I have the unique distinction of co-

143

habitating with the only Ph.d (in Native Education) student, Mohawk cheerleader in the Canadian Football League, possibly in the National Football league too. Now there's a unique combination worthy of *Ripley's Believe It or Not*. And the truly bizarre thing is, Dawn's cheering career is totally unexpected. It's not like she dreamed and dreamed of shaking her pom-poms for tens of thousands of strange people. Not exactly a common career goal for the vast majority of Native youth.

It was just a case of Dawn being at the right place at the right time, being invited to an audition and going just out of curiosity (having seven years dance training behind you doesn't hurt) and having a willingness to shower with several dozen other women (wait a minute... actually that was another letter I sent to Santa).

But perhaps one of the greatest moments of my life was when Dawn and eleven other women were invited as models in the official Argo Cheerleaders calender. She and the rest were going to be flown down to the Dominican Republic for the photography shoot. And for this luxury and privilege, she was going to have to trade in her cheerleading outfit for a bikini, as were the other girls.

So, as logic would dictate, she along with the rest were required to appear for fittings at a Bikini warehouse, so they could find the perfect two outfits that met with approval from the photographer and organizers. And as I said before, I must have done something really cool in a previous life because... I got to go along for the fitting.

So picture it in your mind. A room full of a dozen beautiful women, trying on at least a dozen bikinis in the search for the right "look." I was in awe. Every ten minutes I went up to Dawn and enthusiastically told her, from the bottom of my heart, "Thank you. Really, I mean it Dawn. Thank you. Can I buy you a car or something?" There was another boyfriend at the fitting and I vaguely remember asking him "Have you ever felt completely out of place, but didn't give a damn?" With a sort of glazed look in his face, he agreed. I think he agreed. I may have had that same glazed look too.

I know that to some, this all might seem a bit sexist but they need not worry. I'm a happy camper because I'm just as infatuated with Dawn's Ph.D capabilities as much as her bikini aptitudes. I can say that with complete honesty. But writing an article about a group of people in a room measuring I.Q.'s just doesn't have the same visual stimulus. I would have felt completely out of place there too, but then I would have given a damn.

And in my defense, I remember this one woman I knew who used to criticize men for ogling and drooling over pretty women. Until I finally pointed out a post card of muscle-bound men stuck to her refrigerator door. Oddly enough, the heads had all been cut off the men leaving just their muscular bodies for visual appearance, and I remember her saying that's how she liked her men, great bodies, don't bother about their heads. Two wrongs don't make a right but I rest my case.

So now, after these wonderful experiences have been committed to memory, I think I can safely say that I am now willing to face death, should it ever come. Even face it with a smile. Definitely a huge smile. Though I sure wish I knew what I did that was so wonderful in that last life.

WEAVING THE WEB:
SASKATOON KEY NOTE ADDRESS

The concept of education is a very interesting subject. I was once asked by a very curious and rather intense woman, whom I believe was involved in some Education course somewhere, what I thought education was, from the perspective of an Aboriginal writer. I paused for a moment, in deep thought, thinking to myself, "education, education, hmmm.... what is education?" before finally responding with the best answer I could come up with.

"It's a noun, I believe." I felt it was a highly accurate answer but I guess the humour was lost on her. I thought it was funny. What other answer would you expect from a writer?

If I was an academic, I would probably respond with some-thing overly pontificatious like "Education is the constant absorption, understanding and utilization of information obtained from the world around us." A noun is shorter and says just about as much. Let them absorb, understand and utilize that. I find people tend to over-mysticize subjects. I believe all the really important stuff in life is disgustingly simple.

That is why I always find it odd when I am asked to speak at education conferences like this, for I assure you, I am a very unlikely poster boy for Native education. I failed French in Grade Eleven, for what I feel was a gross miscarriage of justice. Chez Helene would have passed me. *Mon souer est une grun oise...* or something like that. But I digress.

In the almost four decades I have spent walking this earth, I have yet to fulfill my mother's dream – that of attending, and completing the wonderful institution known as University. Yes, I admit it, I am a member of the gainfully uneducated, the cerebrally untrained. I hope you'll all still go to my plays and read my articles. I have it on good authority that, Me good writer. Honest Injun.

Instead of being BIOC, (Big Indian On Campus), I had opted to buy a house with my now ex-girlfriend, which is often, believe it or not, cheaper than a university education. But she was in the midst of completing her PHD in Native Education - Oral Narrative. Can you smell the irony? I found it easier to live vicariously through her academic thrills than rise for those early morning classes or boring keynote addresses.

But this is what truly kills me. As a student, she actually wrote more material, pumped out more written words in any given week, than I would get done in a year. And she didn't get paid for a single word of it. In fact, she had to pay some institution for the privilege of writing all that stuff. See, I'm not smart enough to know that. I always thought that most people should get paid for what they write. I'd make a very bad University student. Silly me. But again, I digress.

I did, however, put in a few years at a college. My reason for attending community college instead of university...? You must keep in mind that in Ontario, we have the option, up until next year, of remaining in high school till Grade Thirteen, and then heading directly off to university. I instead opted for a more speedy exit from my home community of Curve Lake, Ontario to Toronto for college.

The specific reason? Again, not a complicated one. My mother is the oldest of fourteen in a small Reserve with a population of about 800 at that time. So, as a result, by the age of eighteen, I was acutely aware of the simple fact that I was related to every single girl on the Reserve. So I heard Toronto beckoning, where I was related to practically no one. I admit, it's definitely not one of the more inspiring journeys in search of higher education but you must admit, it is highly understandable. Just yesterday I arrived from Lethbridge where it is a common saying that in order to find an unrelated marriage partner, you must travel to at least three provinces away.

With that said, times have changed. It's important to keep in mind that almost half the Aboriginal population in Canada is under twenty-five years of age, thus education becomes of even more importance than when I was that age. The world of education has changed before our very eyes. Stuff that I, and I'm assuming most of you, couldn't imagine, are now the mainstays of classroom life. As one Elder was quoted as saying, "We must go from being hunters in the forest to being hunters in the city."

Computers... what can I say about computers that hasn't already been said, written or discussed. They run the world. I am not sure who are the masters anymore. I remember way back when... I would also like to point out how disturbing it is to me these days that I can say that phrase..." I remember way back when..." without bursting into tears or feeling like my grandfather. Chief Dan George once said something to the effect that he was born in the stone age and would die in the space age. In fifty years, the entire universe changed for somebody of that generation. For us, it is changing quicker. For instance, computer programs... they can become obsolete in a scant year or two.

I had a conversation not that long ago with two young gentlemen, easily in their mid-twenties, who had their own computer animation program in Toronto. We were talking about the fluidity of computer programs and how quickly they change and improve. I told them of the animated movie *Toy Story*, and how one of the animators said that in the time it took to make the film, the technology and software had changed so much that they could have finished the movie in a third less time if they had the same software at the beginning of the production, that was available by the end of the production. Now that's scary.

Then these two young gentlemen told me that every four or five months in their small company, they have to upgrade their systems to keep up with the industry standards, and then take two weeks off for these computer geniuses to retrain and learn the new systems themselves. Every four or five months. Now that's really scary. I am a dinosaur and I have met my asteroid.

But again, I digress. As I was saying earlier, I remember

way back when it seemed the Aboriginal communities next great threat came over the airwaves. Thirty or forty years ago, the Native education community was desperately trying to fight or limit the negative influence television and radio was having on Aboriginal languages.

I remember reading a report several years back that states, in the next thirty years or so, there will only be three Indigenous languages still spoken in Canada; Ojibway, Cree and Inuktituk. Mostly because of the influence of radio and television. I cannot even begin to think what the internet is going to do to that percentage. But maybe I'm being a pessimist. Perhaps this could be a good thing. I have heard that these new technologies could also be the saviour of the dying languages. As with any information and technology, it's what you do with it that's important. Email in Cree syllabics...? I'm sure it's more than possible. I'm sure it's out there somewhere.

Speaking as a writer again, the primary literary references that kept popping up in books and pop culture during my generation, came primarily from either the Bible or Shakespeare. Today, *Star Trek* and *The Simpsons* seem to be the cultural icons that have saturated Canadian and the world's society. It's gone from the written word to the televised spoken word. What will these children of today you teach have to face when they get to be our age and utter those death defying words "I remember way back when..."?

Will they be regaling their children with anecdotes about *This Hour Has 22 Minutes*, Barenaked Ladies, and *North of Sixty*? And how Granny and Grandpa used to play bingo, read a magazine called People, and pay good money to see some hack playwright talk about something he knows nothing about. The future does indeed seem bleak.

But regardless of all the statistics facing us about the state of Canada's financial, social, and educational future, we must continue to view the future with utopian rather than dystopian ideals. Our youth demands it. Being an educator, like being a firefighter or a doctor, by the very definition of the word, is a positive thing. Otherwise, what would be the point? How would you earn those lavish salaries you enjoy? The children you teach are perhaps the first generation of Native youth that has the world at its fingertips. And their hands must be strong enough to hold it.

My youth was not as educationally blessed. As a child I read extensively. Perhaps too much. Books were my life. Yes I admit it, I was a geek! A geek amidst a village of jocks. So much a reading geek that my grandparents once told my mother, though she denies it today, that she shouldn't let me read so much because it wasn't right... what ever "right" means? I guess I'm still not "right." But from all that reading I did over the years, I did discover, later in life, a wonderfully true axiom that I will share with you and everybody should remember. It goes something like this: Jocks get fat. Geeks get rich.

I also remember way back when, as something to do one boring summer, somebody suggested I write an article about the recent band election for a Native newspaper. Having nothing better to do when you're sixteen with no car, I did. I proudly showed it to my mother and she said very distinctly to me, "Why do you want to be a writer, it's not going to get you anywhere?" It's not going to get me anywhere... I still remember those words.

Well, look now, Mom, I'm here in downtown Saskatoon! I'm sure everybody in this room will agree that Saskatoon is definitely somewhere. To this day I love sending her postcards from all the places I get to visit, as a writer; Fiji, New Zealand, Germany, Italy, Lethbridge... Next month I'm leaving for Belgium and Germany again. Granted it's not Saskatoon, but I hear it might be fun.

On top of that, in Grade ten, I remember having my first real flirtation with the concept of being a writer. Curious about the possibilities, I approached my English teacher wondering aloud if it was possible to make a living from creative writing. I still remember it clearly, he was rooting around in the bottom drawer of a filing cabinet in the corner of the classroom, and without even looking up, he said nonchalantly... "no." It was at least another eight or maybe nine years before I again entertained the idea of becoming a writer.

In fact, the very idea that I am a playwright never ceases to amaze my mother and I. Several years back, I had a play produced in Montreal, and I was home on my Reserve when a package arrived from the theatre containing a mass of reviews. My mother and I sat there for about fifteen minutes reading these embarrassingly positive reviews. And my dear sainted mother, who's first language is Ojibway and never had the opportunity for much formal education in life, and who has spent most of her life cooking and cleaning for other people, looked at me in amazement, and said "Where did this come from?" I guess meaning the fact that I was a fairly successful playwright.

And I answered her as truthfully as I could. "I don't know," I told her. Growing up on the Reserve, attending grades one through three there, then being bussed off the Reserve to a nearby white town with all the other Native students, certainly didn't provide me the world at my fingertips. At that time, I thought all playwrights were dead white people. Thinking now that they can also be living Native people says so much for how far our society has come in the last decade or so. Native playwrights, Native lawyers and judges, Native teachers, a Native television Network... maybe the future doesn't look so bleak after all.

So thank you all for allowing me to ramble on here in front of everybody, sharing some errant ideas and casual reminisces from years gone by. From the minute we open our eyes, to the minute we finally close them for good, we are constantly learning something. That is education. Have I learned anything here today...? Well, that's an entirely different speech. Thank you all and have a fabulous conference. And don't forget, there'll be an exam at the end of it.

THE PLACES I'VE BEEN, THE THINGS I'VE SEEN
(An Aboriginal Travel Guide)

PLANE, TRAINS AND READINGS

One of the greatest pleasures I enjoy as a writer is doing public readings. Since I became an author back in the years when people sent letters, not Email, and the typewriter was not a museum piece, I have had the privilege of lecturing/reading across Canada (a g'zillion times), numerous trips to the States, and even New Zealand, Italy (three times) and Germany (five times and counting). It's a chance to see the country or countries, meets new friends and old ones, and make sure the world knows you're a writer. Oh yeah, and sell a few books.

But to quote an old saying, sometimes it is possible to have too much of a good thing. While I really enjoy doing what I do and hope to do it long after it's discovered Stockwell Day is an alien, there are limits to everything. And if you do something long enough, you are bound to have horror stories, no matter how much fun your job is.

Frequently, in order to make out-of-town readings more economical, organizations adopt the philosophy that "the more the merrier... meaning we can split the costs with two or three other organizations and save us a few bucks." It's like getting a taxi from town to the Reserve, it's easier if you get a bunch of people to share the expense.

So it's not uncommon that when I show up in Saskatoon, Winnipeg or some other town eager for some serious, Aboriginal drama or journalism, I find myself facing a large and continuous series of readings, sometimes one right after the other, in a remarkably short period of time, usually at Universities or colleges. I hate to break this news to you out there in the real world but I am what you are paying the universities for. And I thank you.

Recently in Vancouver, I found myself having to do six readings in four days, three on one day alone. Other times, like when I lecture in Germany or am on a book tour, the routine is simply you travel during the day, do a reading at night, grab a quick dinner, sleep in a hotel, get up the next morning trying to figure out if this is Berlin or Regina, then start travelling again for the next stop in the next town. It's the literary equivalent of being a rock star on tour. Without the groupies, money or drugs.

What's even more embarrassing, I'm afraid to say, is when people are scheduled to pick you up at the airport for a lecture, and you walk right by them or they walk right by you because they are attempting to recognize you by the picture on a book that was taken three hairstyles and more than likely a dozen or so pounds ago. "Wow, you don't look anything like your picture" they invariably say, holding up a much younger, better lit photograph. That's when the weeping usually starts.

Pretty soon, you reach a point somewhere between the plane and the classroom where, simply put, you get pretty tired of talking about yourself and your work. You become boring to yourself. Yes, it is possible and it has happened to me several times. I find myself in an English Lit class in Calgary on my way to Kamloops... or was it Victoria... it may have been Halifax, looking at all these young faces who think I know what I'm talking about, reading from my book *The Bootlegger Blues* for the six thousand four hundred and eighteenth time, and I want to stop in the middle of my fourteenth lecture of the month and scream out to the world "Enough about me. So, tell me about you."

Another unusual side-effect is the large number of shirts and sweaters that have been given to me from the various establishments of higher education, as a gift to thank me. The contents of my closet now consists of clothing from Loyalist, Queen's, San Diego State, Nippissing, Simon Fraser, Penn State, UBC... to name just a few. It's not that I mind receiving these wonderful gifts, it's kept me warm most winters and I love the souvenirs of my travels. It's just unnerving when you realize your wardrobe is better educated than you are.

And on the road, you frequently run into somebody who says "Hey, I've read your book!" It's very flattering but you stand there waiting for clarification because you have been lucky enough to have had eleven books published and you would like a few more specifics, like maybe which particular book are they talking about, before you launch into a conversation about its pros and cons. Or I walk by somebody in a crowd and they yell out "hey funny, you don't look like one!" referring to the title of a popular book of mine, probably the one that the previous person had read. I still haven't figured out how to respond to that.

But the thing I find the most uncomfortable yet flattering, is in practically every crowd, there's always somebody who wants you to read something of theirs. I've had people thrust file folders full of poetry at me (and unfortunately I know less about poetry than about Matthew Coon Comb's sex life). Short stories, plays, screenplays, one person even wanted advice on how to turn a twelve line poem into a two hour movie. Hope springs eternal I guess. I know and sympathize because I used to do that very same thing too. That is why you are polite and agree to read what ever it is they give you, even though you know you don't really have the time.

There are certain responsibilities in doing what I do. You have to be nice to everybody, no matter what they may say or comment. One young lady Emailed once to tell me that she loves my writing, even though the first article she ever read of mine really grated on her nerves. I guess I should be complimented.

All in all, regardless of these minor comments, it's all very flattering. I love what I do. That's why I do it. And by far the positives out weight the negatives by a thousand times considering the only other career option is learning to say "would you like fries with that?" People going out of their way to listen to your ramblings, ask you questions about something you've written, or tell you they believe in what you're trying to say, really is a wonderful feeling. No doubt about it. And no amount of complaining or grumbling (dare I say I've become crotchety in my old age?), will ever replace that. And after a month of sitting in my Toronto home, I begin to get antsy, and start to wonder when I'll be flying the blue skies of Canada again and where will I land this time.

But if there was one thing I would change, it would involve timing. I do most of my lecturing/appearances/readings between the months of October and late April. That is the normal school year for Universities and Colleges, as well as the theatre season. This is also the coldest time of the year. You may have heard of it. It's called winter. Just once I would like to go to Thunder Bay, Regina, Halifax, in the summer. Sometimes I feel like an American, believing all of Canada is constantly under snow since that's when I normally see most of Canada.

And by the time you read this, I will have made appearances in Whitehorse, Vancouver, Nippissing, London and soon to be off to Germany again as well as Belgium. No doubt, all will be cold but what the hell, springs coming and I need a new wardrobe.

MY FAVOURITE WRITER WENT TO VENICE
AND ALL I GOT WAS THIS LOUSY ARTICLE

I have many friends who live out west, especially in the Prairies. And on occasion, when they see fit to visit Toronto, I have heard more than one say in admiration "The buildings here in Ontario are so old. Everything out west was built in the last seventy years." One of these days, somebody should take them to Venice, Italy.

This is a town that was settled over fifteen hundred years ago on a set of islands, by people trying to hide from the ravages of Atilla the Hun. Evidently they were successful since the city is still there, still possessing enough beauty to amaze these jaded Aboriginal eyes. I and my then *buz'gem* (Ojibway for someone who lets you know when its time to cut the grass and can you go outside and warm up the car, honey?) were in the area giving lectures at a conference and couldn't pass up the opportunity to tour this famous city. And the more I saw of Venice, the more it made me think of home, for several odd reasons.

It was the small things I noticed that made the connections to my childhood more evident. For instance, everybody knows that Venice is a maze of networking canals. It's amazing and so easy to get lost. No cars, no bikes, very few in-line skaters or skateboards because there is a set of stairs leading up to a bridge at least every twenty feet or so. And the lane ways are barely six to ten feet wide at best. So basically, almost twenty feet in any direction, its easy to find a canal. It's a very compact city. And on these canals are primarily two types of boats. The famous Gondolas, as well as the more practical cargo or the equivalent of floating pick up trucks, sort of all purpose vehicles.

On our first day, we were walking along side one of the

canals when a motorized boat slowly passed by. And for a moment, the sound of water lapping against the wall, the immediately recognizable roar of an outboard motor, and the smell of the exhaust, reminded me of crossing Buckhorn Lake back home. Without all the Italians. And no cappuccino.

Another slice of Aboriginal heaven, every where you turned – pasta. Fabulous pasta at that. It's the law in Venice that every restaurant has to be good. But you pay for it. It's the first time I ever bought a six dollar coke! But try as I might, and trust me I looked, no matter where I went, or how many restaurants I frequented, no where was there to be found anything vaguely resembling what I call the Aboriginal Manna from heaven – macaroni and tomatoes – the building blocks of the Native nation. I'm in Italy, pasta paradise, and there is no elbow Macaroni to be seen. I was severely disillusioned. Not even a single box of Kraft Dinner either.

Some of the restaurants have unusual bathrooms. Instead of toilets, there is a porcelain hole in the ground. I'm not kidding. You stand, lean, or squat, what ever your preference or need, over a large ceramic, what looks like a roasting pan, inlaid into the floor. It was still hooked up to a sewer system, but I remember looking at one thinking that I never thought I would see anything that would make me nostalgic for my childhood outhouse: without the spiders, or catalogues.

Our tour of Venice provided us with numerous other interesting observations of that town. Name another town where you can see a combination pet store and leather shop. One stop shopping I guess. More economical – you save time and money by eliminating the middle man.

Venice is also famous for a type of masquerade ball they have. In fact, every second tourist shop sells a special type of ornate mask known as a Venetian mask, which along with a black cape, is the costume *de jour* at certain celebrations of the year. If you've seen the Tom Cruise/Stanley Kubrick film *Eyes Wide Shut*, you've seen examples of the style. We browsed in the shop that supplied those outfits to the film. We thought we looked better than Tom Cruise and Nicole Kidman. It must have been the masks.

And perhaps most ironic of all, we discovered that a man all Canadians are familiar with, especially the repercussions he brought to all the Native people here, was born in Venice. John Cabot, born Giovanni Caboto, started his seafaring life amongst the canals of Venice and found his way west to "discover" Newfoundland in 1497. Columbus and Caboto – an Italian conspiracy to flood the world with pasta. Or maybe they were just after our tomatoes, unknown in Europe at the time, to revolutionize their cooking. I smell an elaborate plot. As my *buz'gem* said so elegantly, "are we talking... Venice the Menace"?

But what truly amazed us were the amazing Catholic churches we visited both in Venice and the surrounding areas. I had never seen such grandiose, ornate, elaborate and immense buildings of worship in my life. They truly have to be seen to be believed. Anything less than three or four hundred years old were hardly worth mentioning. These incredible structures easily towered above most of the surrounding community.

It reminded me of a trip I once took hiking on Indian reservations in Arizona and New Mexico. Often, in the most isolated and poorest villages, the largest, most well built building in the village was always the Catholic Church. In one community, everything but the Church was constructed of adobe and dried mud. But the hundred year old Church itself was fabricated from huge stone blocks and massive wooden beams that had to be transported by man and horse over sixty miles. But that's nothing – some churches in Europe took over a hundred years to complete the construction due to their size and elaborate architecture.

It can make one theorize that the whole Protestant Reformation had nothing to do with religious dogma or corruption. But that it was instigated by people who were just too damn tired to keep building these massive churches. That's probably why Protestant churches are so modest.

In the end, we had a marvelous, unforgettable time. All

except for one minor detail. As fabulous as Venice was, there was one other town we felt a primal, First Nations urge to visit. A town with the same name as the fundamental force that permeates a large portion of Reserve life. When we were in Germany, we visited the other two towns in the Holy Trinity of Aboriginal meats, Hamburg and Frankfurt. But only in Italy, exists the mecca of the Native culinary world, and we were a few scant hours from it. But for some reason, try as we might, the Gods did not provide us with the opportunity to pay homage and worship at this sacred sight.

But in every Native person's heart, regardless of their tribe, there is the dream to make a pilgrimage to the holy town of Bologna.

And God willing, someday we will return to that alter. And pray.

ADVENTURES IN WHITEHORSE

When I told people I was going to Whitehorse, I got a blank stare. "In January?" was often the only comment I got. Yes, in January, but I didn't mind the unusual responses because in a way, it all made sense. Especially since I was going up north to attend the first annual Whitehorse Comedy Festival. And when ever I think of people going to Whitehorse in January, I burst out laughing.

One always expects the worse when traveling up north but I was in for a rude awakening. The climate and atmosphere when we arrived were both quite warm. The temperature hovered just below the freezing point and everybody was excited about the upcoming Festival. People were going out of their way to make it special. I came to screen my documentary on Native humour, along with several comedians, improv artists, actors and general all around funny people eager to prove their stuff. Everybody was expecting a fabulous time.

Granted it took some time to get used to the $15.00 breakfasts. Breakfasts that were in the dark. The sun didn't rise 'till about 10:00 every morning, for a paltry five or six hours of shining. Welcome to the North.

Don't get me wrong. Whitehorse is a fabulous and interesting town, but like any community in Canada, you sometimes have to pay a little more attention to the details to find the more unusual aspects of the population. For instance, the waitress at the hotel restaurant casually told us over our bacon and eggs (did I mention the $15.00?) that she had originally trained to be a mortician but then decided to go into hotel management. I guess she liked working with people.

On arriving, the Festival co-ordinators gave each participant a contact sheet with a list of important phone numbers we might need during the next few days. Stuff like transportation, Festival organizers, restaurants, venues etc. Then at the bottom was the number for Ashley and Alexis, Professional Escorts (discretion assured). Three thoughts went through my mind. First of all, how wonderfully... liberal the Festival and Whitehorse was to not only have escorts but to include them in the festival information package. Darned civilized I thought.

And secondly, in a town of ten or twenty thousand people, all of whom probably know each other, how can you promise "discretion assured"? It's a small town! You're walking down the street with Alexis and people are pointing and giggling. "Look who Alexis is with tonight!" or "Hey Ashley, say hello to your mother for me." So I wondered if the term "discretion assured" was false advertising.

And thirdly, when did I get my per diem money?

But perhaps my most memorable adventure in the Yukon was the invitation I received to go "mushing" or to the untrained southerner, dog sledding. I had never done it but decided to brave the elements for yet another tall tale to tell the grandchildren should my girlfriend ever stop wearing flannel to bed.

This event took place about forty minutes outside of town at a hot springs. Several of us stood around, watching the owners unload and harness the animals. The dogs were barking, jumping around, excited to be out on the land and eager to start running. It was controlled, though loud, bedlam. It was then that I said the unsayable. Amidst the crying and yelping dogs, I turned to some nearby friends and proceeded to sing the popular song "Who Let the Dogs out! Hoo hoo hoo hoo hoo." Suddenly, there was silence, and then one person hung his head low muttering to himself "Somebody had to say it. You knew somebody was going to say it." Luckily I managed to talk them out of leaving me behind.

Feeling very Jack Londonish, I eagerly pulled out my cell to call my girlfriend. As I started to tell her enthusiastically what I was about to do, the owner started laughing. She knew I was

Native and here I was, in the Yukon north, talking to my girl-friend in Toronto on a cell phone, acting like a little boy about to go off in his first pony ride, she commented that the spirits of my noble ancestors weren't exactly flowing up from the ground into my heart announcing "This is the proud legacy we have left behind." Perhaps I need to get out more.

So I eagerly jumped into my sled and off we went on our merry adventure. That was just before it tipped over and I went sliding into a snow bank. I don't remember that being in the original contract with the festival. Evidently sleds and dogs are like cars or planes. They each have their own feel. And the guy driving mine had never driven this team or sled before and wasn't familiar with it's nuances. Nor was he familiar with his passenger spitting up snowballs.

But one of the most important reasons I and most people travel is to learn. To accumulate facts and experiences which will hopefully make our lives richer. And on this trip, I did learn something very important. Something I will pass on to those grandchildren somewhere down the road. I will tell them "Listen closely. Never, ever, ever, go to a festival of any sort, that is co-sponsored by a brewery. It is evil. Pure evil. I hadn't played a game of caps in years and I was surprised how quickly it came back. At three in the morning, I barely got out of Whitehorse alive."

I'm still waiting for the hotel to send me the dirty laundry I forgot to bring home.

COLUMBUS MERELY HAD A BETTER PUBLICIST

It's generally accepted that the Vikings and Columbus were the first to visit the shores of our beloved Turtle Island, "discovering" all of us savages in the process of building monumental cities, developing complex social and political structures, creating amazing works of art, and suffering from the delusion that anybody who had a God that had written "thou shall not kill" or "thou shall not steal", might actually be worth inviting to stay for dinner. Unfortunately, the vast majority of the European population at that time couldn't read. And it showed. It's amazing how much trouble a simple boat can get you into.

Modern scholars, however, now concede that perhaps the Vikings and Columbus were not the first to darken our eastern (or western) shores. Evidence exists supporting the claim that, in fact, there were a multitude of non-Turtle Island residents sharing tea and bannock with our grandfathers and grandmothers in the last five thousand years.

The following is a list of eight possible explorations of our noble land by non-Italian or Nordic heritage.

Hsi and Ho (c.2640 BC)

It is argued that these two Imperial Chinese astronomers were ordered by their Emperor to make studies of lands to the East of China. The two men sailed north to the Bering Strait, then south along the North American coastline, spending time with the Pueblo in the Grand Canyon, and eventually journeying to Mexico and Guatemala.

Votan and Wixepecocha (c.800–400 BC)

According to Hindu legends, Hindu missionaries sailed from India, and island hopping, made their way to Central and South America. Votan, a trader, lived amongst the Mayans as a historian and his contemporary, Wixepecocha, was a Hindu priest who settled with the Zapotecs of Mexico.

Hui Shun (458 AD)

Official Chinese documents propose a Buddhist monk named Hui Shun, accompanied by four Afghan disciples, sailed from China to Alaska, then continued his journey down the coast by foot. Reaching Mexico, he preached Buddhism to Central Americans, supposedly naming Guatemala in honour of Gautama Buddha. He returned to China after forty years.

St. Brendan (c 550 AD)

Two medieval manuscripts tell of the journey of an Irish priest, who with seventeen other monks, sailed west from Ireland in a leather hulled boat. They supposedly traveled as far as Newfoundland and the Caribbean.

The Albans (8th Century)

According to Farley Mowat's book, The Farfarers, these Scottish sea people not only settled Iceland and Greenland centuries before the Vikings, they also had a thriving and extensive trade and business arrangements with the Indigenous people of Baffin Island, Labrador and Newfoundland.

Prince Madog Ab Owain Gwynedd (1170 & 1190 AD)

Due to political conflicts with his brothers, this Welsh prince sailed west from Wales and landed somewhere in the Americas where he built and fortified a settlement. After several years he returned to Wales, leaving behind 120 men. He crossed the Atlantic again in 1190 to discover the settlement destroyed and all his men had been annihilated.

King Abubakari II (1311 AD)

After learning from Arab scholars that there was land to the West of the Atlantic, King Abubakari, a Muslim from Mali, became obsessed with extending his kingdom across the ocean and ordered the creating of a fleet to sail to this unclaimed land. It is believed they landed in Panama, traveled south, and settled in the Incan Kingdom.

Johannes Scolp and Joao Vaz Corte Real (1476 AD)

Portugal and Denmark arranged a mutual expedition to find the fabled sea route to China. The combined fleet sailed across the Atlantic, exploring Labrador, Hudson's Bay, St. Lawrence River and the Gulf of St. Lawrence. Failing to find a route to China, they quickly returned to Europe where their discoveries were ignored.

It seems everybody was trying to get here. A word of advice, next time you're at the beach, keep watching that horizon. No telling who's next.

DEEP IN THE HEART OF WINNIPEG

Just last month I had the privilege of spending several fabulous days in the heart of wonderful downtown Winnipeg. I had been to Winnipeg many times in the past, have many wonderful and close friends living somewhere in its depths, but I had never visited under these auspicious circumstances. I was an invited guest at the Winnipeg International Author's Festival! I felt like an adult – one with a free plane ticket.

At this literary festival, authors from all over the world were there to read from their latest brilliant works, generate some publicity, hob nob with other fellow writers (what ever a hob nob is – I think its a small furry animal that lives somewhere up in the Arctic), and sample the hospitality of this prairie city. During the Festival, I met some great people, ate some wonderful food, and generally left the province with many more magnificent memories to tell the kids (should I ever have any – mental note: casually bring up this issue with girlfriend, she may have input).

But as with everything in life, you must take the bad with the good. And much like the newspapers, we often tend to remember and report the not-so-great occurrences. For instance, I learned an important lesson about Winnipeg and its festivals, they really put you to work in this town. In the incredibly short time of a scant forty–eight hours, I did nine, maybe ten readings – it got fuzzy after a while. After about the fifth or sixth reading, I even found myself boring.

On top of that, I was there to promote my new book, a collection of humorous essays and articles titled *Further Adventures of a Blue-eyed Ojibway: Funny You Don't Look Like One ~~Too~~ Two*. In fact, a book launch was planned for my final night in Winnipeg. One minor problem. No book. It seems the company that printed the books had problems somewhere in the process which resulted in no book for the launch. Now, I cannot speak for most people but when I go to a book launch, generally I'm expecting to see a book. Call me a radical but that is what I have been conditioned to expect. The result – one cancelled book launch and one depressed writer. Not Hemingway depressed, more Lord Byron depressed.

But that still left me with the nine readings I already mentioned. Nine readings that none of my dozen or so friends in Winnipeg bothered to attend. But I'm not bitter. Really. I'm sure they had nine other separate things to do.

Then things took a different tack. At two of these readings I had the pleasure of working with Greg Scofield, the noted Métis poet. We were both at an inner-city high school, reading and answering questions from the student body. First Greg got asked this question by a young man hidden somewhere in the audience, then it was my turn to answer the question while on the stage. "Have you ever tried to kill yourself?"

Both of us hemmed and hawed, awed I think by the blasé-nature in the delivery of the question. It's not everyday one gets asked a question like that, by a teenage audience, at a reading. I remember blurting out an answer, my mind reeling with what would motivate a sixteen year old to ask such a question, twice in the same day, the same hour.

I remember responding to the suicide question with some half-hearted joke about, "only when I open my American Express bill," but even then I knew I wasn't doing the inquiry justice. I was probably just deflecting the uncomfortableness of it. In my travels I've been to Davis Inlet and a host of other communities where suicide is a real and ever present issue. My second answer of simply "no," seemed to pale beside the ramifications of the question.

I spent the rest of that day, in between other readings, thinking about that teenager's question. Perhaps Greg had a better perspective for answering. In his recently published autobiography, *Thunder Through My Viens*, he talks quite freely about some of the harrowing times he's gone through and how he has managed to survive the darker times. I have such great respect for people who have gone through that and come out the other end. That which does not destroy us, makes us stronger. The German philosopher Neitzche had it right I guess.

I hope that Neitzche is on the course list at that school.

HOW TO PLANT A LEGEND

I've been a bad boy. A very bad boy. And if I'm lucky, it won't come back to haunt me. And to all the Native people out there who travel the world, it was just meant as a joke. Really.

The name of the country is Belgium. Brussels to be exact. I was there at a theatre conference lecturing about the wonders of Aboriginal theatre in Canada. One of the organizers, a lovely older Jewish lady, offered to take my girlfriend at the time and myself out sightseeing. So sitting at a picturesque cafe, drinking really strong European coffee, she asked us if Native people celebrated any traditional holidays or seasonal ceremonies. My ex-girlfriend instantly began to regale her with a proud litany of Iroquoian rites. Then this curious lady asked me about Ojibway examples.

I don't know why, but for some reason, perhaps the innate Trickster in me, I answered "Well, it's a little known fact that the most respected and revered holiday in the Ojibway year marks the death of Elvis Presley." She looked confused for a second before nodding in sympathy and respect. Sitting next to her, my ex-girlfriend rolled her eyes (did you know you can actually hear eyes rolling in their sockets if they're done with enough annoyance?).

And for some reason I don't remember, the conversation continued quickly in another direction and Elvis' elevated position in the Ojibway pantheon of ceremonies gave way to other fascinating conversation. I never did get the opportunity to correct my failed attempt at humour. Now I am back in Canada with a guilty conscience and possibly responsible for a growing, if inaccurate legend. So now this woman, who is a respected member of the University of Brussels, attached to a department that teaches/studies Canadian theatre, now thinks Ojibways have an un-natural attachment to Elvis Presley. And the scary thing is, she might not be that far off.

In this new millennium, I still occasionally see older Native men walking down Rez roads, sporting what looks like vintage ducktail hair styles – heavily slicked back, listening to classic rock n' roll music, and wearing clothes that would have seemed outdated the day the music died. In many Native communities it's called "The Time Warp" effect, ancient cars, outhouses right next to the satellite dish, copies of *People* magazine read by women who still cover their hair with colourful handkerchiefs.

And, I'm ashamed to say, this isn't the first time I have been known to bend the cultural truth a little when pressed. A long time ago, a fellow Ojibway friend and I decided one summer that we had time to kill and money to spend. With that extremely rare revelation, we found ourselves several months later in New Zealand, hanging out with the Maori, the Indigenous people of that far off South Pacific island.

After several weeks with one particular family, that of the noted Maori author Patricia Grace, we were faced with an unusual dilemma. A challenge was thrown to us. This cultural exchange was a little one sided. Since we had lived with them, shared in the Maori lifestyle, ate Maori foods, this family was curious to sample North American, specifically Ojibway cuisine. So here we were, two Ojibways with our culinary backs against a wall, in a land where lamb and red pickled beets rule. How does one prepare a traditional Ojibway meal under such conditions? Head to the Zoo and see if there are any deer or moose handy? Not to mention my corn soup talents are a little rusty.

Our solution!? The tasty and nutritional food that has raised many a generation of Ojibway and still continues to grace our Indigenous kitchen tables. These humble Maori were treated to the unique delicacy known as Macaroni and Tomatoes or also known as, depending where you come from, hangover soup. Two huge pot fulls. One robust Maori had three bowls full. That is one of the proud Ojibway legacies we left behind.

I try and reason to myself that I'm not all that inaccurate or evil. Elvis did actually have some Native blood I'm told. Cherokee I think. But in America that's like saying politicians occasionally lie. And tomatoes are actually Native (no pun intended) to the Americas. But maybe that's stretching it a bit.

So to all those who may visit other places on this fabulous planet, don't be surprised at what you may hear about the Ojibway where ever you may go. It's a colourful world out there and evidently I'm doing my bit to make it a little bit more colourful. It comes from having a creative spirit. I guess I won't even begin to tell you what I told the Cubans and the Fijians. I think it may have dealt with us being the best lovers or something like that. And that every Thursday was "Take An Ojibway To Lunch Day." I wish!

I just wish I could remember when Elvis' birthday really was. Should this woman ever come to Canada, I may have to arrange something pretty quick.